JAMES KIRKE PAULDING

JAMES KIRKE PAULDING (1778–1860)
At the age of Sixty-five

Copy of an engraving by F. Halpin from a medallion by J. G. Chapman

JAMES KIRKE PAULDING

VERSATILE AMERICAN

BY

AMOS L. HEROLD, Ph.D.

Professor and Head of the English Department
in the University of Tulsa

AMS PRESS, INC.
NEW YORK
1966

Reprinted with the permission of the
Original Publisher, 1966

AMS PRESS, INC.
New York, N.Y. 10003
1966

Manufactured in the United States of America

DEDICATION

To My Friend, Mrs. Jane Cameron Harrison,

and

To the Memory of My Grandfather,
David Vanmeter Ruckman

PREFACE

A proverb reminds us that no man lives to himself, and such biographers as Boswell and Carlyle are recognized as masters partly because they succeeded admirably in presenting their subjects with an appropriate background of contemporary scenes and characters. Keeping this principle in mind while writing a critical biography of James K. Paulding, I have at least endeavored not only to tell the story of his life and varied writings, but also, in some measure, to restore the circumstances, political, social, and literary, in which he lived and worked.

Accordingly, one aim of Chapter I is to reveal what childhood in the New York cradle of liberty was really like; Chapter II seeks to present some aspects of the City of New York as it appeared to Paulding more than a century ago; Chapter III deals with the Salmagundi period of Irving's early popularity; Chapter IV is concerned with the so-called literary war between England and the United States; Chapter V explores an almost virgin field of the early American short story; Chapter VI presents Paulding as the Dutch novelist of the New York Dutch; Chapter VII shows him critical of his own age and yet sharing in the romantic love of nature; and Chapter VIII carries him into Van Buren's cabinet and then to the picturesque home of his old age on the Hudson River.

To several members of the English Department of Columbia University I am gratefully indebted: to Carl

Van Doren for suggesting the subject and for helpful counsel; to Professor William P. Trent, who read the proof
sheets, Professor George P. Krapp, Dr. Samuel L. Wolff in
particular, and Dr. H. M. Ayres for the generous aid of
their counsel and scholarship; to Professor Dixon R. Fox
of the History Department; and to Professor Ashley H.
Thorndike for the kindly interest of an imperturbable
friend.

For innumerable acts of gracious helpfulness I thank the
library officials of Columbia University, the New York
Public Library, the New York Historical Society, the
Library of Congress, the Naval Library of the United
States, Yale University, Harvard University, the Boston
Public Library, Brown University, the Historical Library
of Pennsylvania at Philadelphia, Bucknell University, the
University of Cincinnati, the University of Tulsa, the Tulsa
Public Library, and the British Museum. I thank also the
custodians of the public records at Poughkeepsie, White
Plains, and New York City.

In addition, I owe much to the following persons: to
James K. Paulding Jr. of New York City, grandson of the
author, for helpful suggestions and traditions regarding
his grandfather; to Fred Lewis Pattee, who read the manuscript; to Edgar M. Bacon of Tarrytown, N. Y., George
S. Hellman of New York City, and Nelson F. Adkins, a
graduate student at Yale and author of a forthcoming life
of Fitz-Greene Halleck, for clues to original material; to
my friends, Dr. O. S. Coad, Dr. Jane Louise Mesick, and
Dr. John O. Beaty, for aid or advice; to Mrs. A. L. Herold,
my wife, and my sisters, Reta L. and Lula B. Herold; to
my friend, Mrs. Jane C. Harrison of Lewisburg, Pennsylvania, for the use of her private library and the pleasure

of writing part of the work in her hospitable home; and to the revered memory also of that estimable gentleman, now deceased, Dr. John H. Harris, cheerful philosopher, powerful speaker, and for thirty years president of Bucknell University.

AMOS L. HEROLD.

University of Tulsa,
October, 1926.

CONTENTS

CONTENTS

LIST OF ILLUSTRATIONS

JAMES KIRKE PAULDING

CHAPTER I

IN THE CRADLE OF LIBERTY

1. *Preliminary*

AMONG the non-English colonists that entered into the composition of the American people, the Dutch of New Netherland were numerous and influential. Though, after the English conquest of 1664, they were a subject people, whose customs and language and literature were slowly displaced by those of the conquerors, yet Dutch honesty, industry, economy, and imagination continued to honor American history. Among their descendants were two presidents, Martin Van Buren and Theodore Roosevelt, such early authors as Gulian C. Verplanck and James Kirke Paulding, and the more recent Walt Whitman and Henry Van Dyke.

It was, moreover, the New York Dutch that inspired Irving's "Rip Van Winkle" and "The Legend of Sleepy Hollow," and elicited his comic masterpiece, *A History of New York* by Diedrich Knickerbocker. But, delightful and renowned as these works are, they are not authentic records of the Dutch. It is no disparagement of Irving to state that by ancestry, association, and temperament, he was not qualified to penetrate to the heart of the New York Dutch. His parents were English; he grew up in an Anglo-American atmosphere; and like a traveler, he viewed the Dutch from the outside. For the most part he found in them only materials to nourish his comic imagination; with the most kindly and charitable feeling for his subjects, he yet produced a travesty upon them, amusing for its exaggeration and absurdity. Rip Van Winkle's "insuperable aversion to all kinds of profitable labor" and Mynheer Van Tassel's rural munificence, if true, were exceptional and magnified by the rich imagination of the author, who wrote the tales while living in England and dreaming of his boyhood home in New York.

Without detracting in the least from Irving's well-deserved and well-established fame as a humorous historian of the Dutch, the present study, among other subordinate purposes, undertakes to show that the early American author, James Kirke Paulding, belongs to the New York Dutch; that he was distinguished for his versatility, independence, and staunch Americanism; and that, because of his tales and novels, he deserves to be remembered as the chief Dutch interpreter of the New York Dutch.

An examination of Paulding's life and writings begins with the Saratoga period of the American Revolution, continues through the critical years before and after the adoption of the constitution and the inauguration of Washington, and moves onward through the War of 1812 and the Mexican War to the unmistakable rumblings of the contest between the States. But, fortunately, in the long and eventful period of Paulding's maturity, the god of war interfered little with the normal and healthy development of the American Republic. In the main, it was a peaceful and prosperous era. The astounding growth of the City of New York typified that of the nation; Jefferson's purchase of the vast and potentially rich Louisiana Territory stimulated and fortified its expansion. American necessities and ingenuity mothered the invention of the cotton gin, the steamboat, the reaper, and the telegraph; and railroads began to replace canals. In Congress and throughout the land there were stormy oratorical and newspaper battles over the problem of slavery, but Gettysburg and Appomattox were safely concealed in the future.

Like his greater English contemporaries, Wordsworth and Landor, Paulding lived to a ripe old age and greeted two generations of American statesmen and authors. As an imaginative boy of ten he probably heard his father read and approve the arguments advanced in *The Federalist* for the adoption of the constitution. When Jefferson in 1800 won the presidency over Aaron Burr in a close contest in the House of Representatives, Paulding was a young man of twenty-two, living in New York City; in 1815 his defence of the United States won an appointment from President Madison; in 1838 he became Secretary of the Navy under President Van Buren. With the rest of the reading world, he saw Scott's poetic star rise in Edinburgh and grow dim in London amid the sheet lightning of Byron's impassioned rhetoric; and he lived to see Dickens, George Eliot, and Hawthorne win the public favor. He shared with Irving the composition and the popularity of *Salmagundi* (1807); in the literary war on British travelers in the United States he won signal honors; and between 1830 and 1840, as a novelist, he rivaled Cooper and Simms. He published some of his prose in the *Southern Literary Messenger* under the editorship of Poe, whose whole literary career he witnessed.

2. *Ancestry*

Late in life Paulding and his son William, owing to what appeared to be conflicting evidence, were in doubt whether the family was originally Dutch or English.

Careful search, however, proves that the family was Dutch. From legal documents still preserved in New York City and at White Plains, and from recently translated and published records of the New York Dutch Reformed Church and of the Old Dutch Church of Sleepy Hollow, one can weave a brief, trustworthy narrative. The Dutch fathers exercised full liberty in spelling their names; in truth, many respectable persons in those ancient days, both male and female, Dutch and English, were content to legalize contracts with their crossmarks, thus happily evading responsibility for inconsistent spelling. The imagination displayed in turning the name of Paulding into English foretold that the family would some day boast a novelist. In the early records the name was spelt Paldinck, Palding, Paaling, Paling, Paalding, Paelding, Palden; the modern form—Paulding—was used first and adhered to by William, the father of James Kirke Paulding.

The ancestor of this family in America was Joost Paldinck, later anglicised as Joseph Palding, though the English equivalent of the Dutch *Joost* is *Justus*. Joost was admitted as a freeman of the City of New York in 1683, and according to a list of the inhabitants of the city prepared in 1703 he was then at the head of a family consisting of one male, one female, four children, one negro, and one negress.[1] From the church record of marriages [2] it appears that Joost was a native of Cassant, Holland, and that he wedded Catharina Dúÿts of New York on April 1, 1688. According to James Riker's *History of Harlem* (N. Y., 1881), Catharina, granddaughter of a Dane nicknamed "great shoe," was only fourteen years old at the time of

---

[1] *Valentine's History of New York*, pp. 357 and 373.

[2] *Marriages, 1639 to 1801, in the Reformed Dutch Church, New York*, published in the Collections of the New York Genealogical and Biographical Society, Vol. 1, p. 64. For baptisms see Vols. 2 and 3.

her marriage. The records of the same church, which the Roosevelts attended, show that between 1689 and 1708 Joost Palding and Catharina his wife presented three sons and five daughters for baptism.

Meanwhile, Joost was prospering in his business as bolter and cordwainer. In 1703 for valuable consideration he bought a tract of land in Westchester County, probably near White Plains, and three years later he sold it for one hundred and twenty pounds.[3] In November, 1705, he lent to Captain Abraham Vanlaer, "fourty-seaven pounds and ten shillings," on double bond and at 16 2/3 per cent interest, for fitting out a sloop to privateer against France or Spain during the War of the Spanish Succession.[4] A widower and resident of Westchester in 1709, he married Zophia Krankheit, widow, of Phillipsburgh (now Tarrytown).[5] While living there, he was deacon and church treasurer in 1712 and 1713, when he submitted a report to the consistory and requested letters of dismissal for himself and family to the Dutch Church of New York. His official record was commended, and the family returned to the City. Thus early the Pauldings, fluctuating between Westchester County and New York City, played an honorable part in colonial life.

Of Joost Paldinck's three sons, two, Abraham, baptized in 1697, and Joost or Joseph Jr., baptized in 1708, reached maturity and left descendants. Abraham prospered in New York City and died there about 1762, leaving a considerable estate to his nine "dear children." Joseph Jr.,

---

[3] Record of Deeds, Westchester Co., Book E, pp. 422–424.

[4] N. Y. City Conveyances, Book 26, p. 61.

[5] *First Record Book of the Old Dutch Church of Sleepy Hollow*, translated by Rev. David Cole, D.D., and published by the Yonkers Historical and Library Association, 1901. Phillipsburgh was thus spelled by Colonel William Paulding.

grandfather of the author, married Susannah White at the Dutch Reformed Church, New York, on June 18, 1732; their oldest child was named Joost (3rd), and their second, William, baptized in December, 1735, became the father of James Kirke, who nearly a century later wrote the following autobiographic letter to an admirer:

"New York, 28th Dec., 1827.

"Dear Sir:

"I thank you for your kind letter and will not fail to send you occasionally any little publications of the day which I think will interest you, desiring no other return but your friendship and good wishes.

"In answer to your friendly enquiries,—I am by the Father's side *pure* Dutch—both my Grandfather and Grandmother, whom I remember, were Dutch—spoke Dutch—and read Dutch out of an Old Dutch Bible with silver corners and silver clasps. By my mother, I am adulterated with some French and English Blood; but I am so far a Dutchman yet, that I hate all interlopers and reverence old customs. My Father was a member of the First Council of State, after the abolition of the British power here, and afterwards Commissary General. What is very remarkable, he ruined himself in this last office, instead of getting rich—by pledging his own credit with the farmers of Westchester and Dutchess, when that of the Government was gone. John Paulding who captured André was the Eldest Son of my Father's Eldest Brother, of course my first Cousin. He was a remarkable man of his class and cut out for a Hero. The recent mayor of this city is my Eldest Brother. Thus you have my pedigree. Tell your Father that, though a little sophisticated, I am a Dutchman all over, and that I have a great respect for the name of De Wit—I don't mean DeWitt Clinton.

"I am *Dr* Sir yours truly,

"J. K. PAULDING." [6]

In 1753 his grandparents, who reared 'five other children, removed from the city to a farm about two miles east of

[6] *History of the City of New York* by Mary L. Booth (1876), Vol. 6, p. 11, 493. An autograph letter inserted in a copy belonging to the New York Public Library, Emmet Collection.

Tarrytown, attended the Dutch Church there, spoke Dutch, conned the pages of their precious old Dutch Bible, and survived the Revolution, the grandfather dying in 1786. Four of his sons, Joseph, William, Peter, and John, served in the Revolutionary Army, and the last three lived to their tenth decade.

William Paulding, the father of James K. Paulding, grew up in New York City, and before he was thirty years of age became commander of several ships sailing to many parts of the world. He had wide experience, and read extensively; in his old days he loved to entertain children with stories of his own adventures or those in the *Arabian Nights*. He married Catharine Ogden, a native of Brunswick, New Jersey, on July 25, 1762, in New York. There two daughters, Catharine and Henrietta, were born. At this time he appears to have become a landsman. About 1767 the family moved to Tarrytown, where William built a large dwelling and storehouse beside the river, on what is now the south-west corner of White and Franklin Streets, opened a store, traded with the farmers, and by 1776 was in comfortable circumstances. Here five children were born: Julia (1768), who married William Irving about 1794 and whose son, Pierre M. Irving, became Washington Irving's aide and biographer; William Paulding (1770), who prospered at the law in New York and served in Congress and as Mayor of New York City; Joseph (1772); Susannah (1774), who died at the age of twenty-three; and Nathaniel (1776), who became a prosperous, generous-hearted wine-merchant in New York.

At this point came the Declaration of Independence, and in August, 1776, William, an active and influential patriot, was appointed Commissary of the New York Militia north of King's Bridge with the rank of Colonel. Late

in 1776, after the battle of White Plains and the approach
of the British, he wisely removed his wife and children
from Tarrytown to Great Nine Partners (then in Dutchess
County, now in Putnam), a safe retreat beyond the American lines, where they remained till the end of the war.
Here in the midst of the stirring events of the Revolution,
his son, James Kirke Paulding, was born on August 22,
1778; and here too, in 1781, was born Euphemia, the
youngest child. Colonel Paulding served throughout the
Revolution, visiting his wife and children during the winter months; with the return of peace he took them back
to his Tarrytown residence, which escaped destruction at
the hands of British marauders because its burning would
have endangered a Tory's house standing nearby.[7]

Through no fault of his own, Col. Paulding's generous
and efficient services as Commissary resulted in his financial ruin and the deep humiliation of imprisonment for
debts he had contracted in getting food for the patriot
army. Serving a makeshift government, which had no
cash and little credit, Paulding at length faced a crisis in
feeding the troops. When the impoverished farmers refused to exchange their products for worthless continental
money or his promises as a public agent, he bravely pledged
his personal fortune, procured the necessary supplies, and
ultimately died a ruined man embittered by the ingratitude of his country. But Paulding did not despair till
all efforts to get compensation from the federal and state
governments had failed. On April 17, 1781, a report of

[7] The three preceding paragraphs are based on Henrietta Paulding
Requa's application for a pension and the birth records from William
Paulding's Bible, preserved in Washington, D. C.; *Souvenir of the
Revolutionary Soldiers' Monument Dedication at Tarrytown, N. Y.*
(1894) compiled by M. D. Raymond; and *Literary Life of James K.
Paulding,* compiled by his own son, William I. Paulding (New York,
1867).

the Board of Treasury brought his application favorably before the Continental Congress, both Jonathan Trumbull and the Board of Treasury acknowledging an obligation of nearly $10,000 and recommending that it be paid.[8]

The business came before the Continental Congress again on April 27, and a year later that body referred the petition of William Paulding to the Superintendent of Finance. There the published record ends. In October, 1784, however, being liable to arrest for the obligations he had assumed, he petitioned the Legislature of the State of New York, submitting a copy of his appointment and requesting that the balance of his accounts be paid in forfeited lands or in any other way acceptable to the state. And the great state which had given a farm to each of Major André's captors granted him no relief.

Colonel Paulding then submitted to the demands of his creditors. They evidently had waited long and were not inconsiderate, but finally they took all his personal property. Then his Tarrytown home on a lot 112 feet square with wharves in the Hudson River was sold to Thomas Randall and Thomas Roach, New York merchants and probably his friends, who in June, 1785, mortgaged the property to the Pauldings for six hundred pounds.[9] Soon afterwards Paulding was arrested for debts still unpaid, and was confined in a log prison at White Plains about six miles east of Tarrytown.

The situation of the mother and nine children may well be imagined. The older boys, William and Joseph, however, she kept in school at Hackensack, New Jersey; Henrietta in 1784 had married Lieutenant Isaac Requa, who continued the mercantile business of his father-in-law, prospered, and was a highly respected citizen and prom-

[8] *Journals of the Continental Congress*, Vol. 19, p. 401.

[9] Record of Mortgages, Westchester Co., Book C, pp. 285–286.

inent local official. Catharine had also married. James, then a small boy of six or eight years, was sent every Saturday on an old borrowed horse to carry to his imprisoned father a supply of clothes and such little comforts and necessaries as the family could afford. For the boy, it was a melancholy journey. Fortunately, after a few months his father was released by the accidental burning of the jail, and was allowed to walk home, where he remained undisturbed by his creditors. "He was a proud man," James later wrote, "and the ingratitude of his country, joined to the disgrace of a prison, though they did not produce despair, so operated on his mind that he ever afterward neglected the means of retrieving his fortune." Yielding to disgust for the world, he resorted to books and newspapers for employment and consolation, and the days of the old patriot rolled on quietly to his ninetieth year.[10]

In view of all the evidence, the validity of the debt that the United States owed Col. William Paulding is unquestioned; the failure to pay it was a miscarriage of justice; and the moral obligation of the government to his descendants still stands. To determine the amount now due is an interesting speculation; bankers can hardly believe their calculations. Nearly ten thousand dollars at six per cent interest compounded annually for a period of 146 years now amounts to many millions of dollars.

In meeting this tragic disaster, which carried away their material resources and benumbed the father's heart and spirit, the mother proved to be the guardian angel of the children and the presiding genius of the family. She triumphed over misfortune and poverty, and in some way paid off the mortgage. Small and symmetrical, black-eyed and clear-headed, light and graceful in her movements so

[10] *Literary Life of James K. Paulding*, pp. 19–21.

that at seventy-eight she used to trip up and down the steep stairs in her home like a girl, she exemplified the truth of an observation that James later made in reference to the mother of Washington:

"A firm, tender, careful, and sensible mother is the greatest blessing that ever fell to the lot of a human being." Of his own mother, he said: "To her conduct I can never do justice. By her thrift, her activity and industry, and by that magic with which some women seem to achieve impossibilities, she managed, with the aid of occasional acts of kindness from her married daughters and her sister in New York, not only to feed and clothe us, but to send us to school, not at the expense of the parish but her own. This she did by plying her needle, morning, noon, and night, with a cheerful alacrity that diffused itself over the whole house. . . . All that I have ever been I owe to her."

Her ambition for her children was largely realized. About 1794 Julia became the wife of William Irving, merchant and public official of New York; William Paulding Jr., after studying law in New York, became there a successful lawyer and politician; Joseph, probably a shipmaster; James K., an author and navy official; as already noted, Susan died early, and of Euphemia no record has been found. A grandson wrote that Mrs. Paulding lived to see all her children comfortable and some of them wealthy and distinguished. She herself had an Indian summer of good fortune. By an unexplained act of the New York Legislature passed on April 9, 1805, she was given a one-fourth share in the real estate of Thomas Roach of New York City. From this property she realized within two years nearly $4200 in cash.[11] And the days of this good and virtuous woman, whose children became her pride and monument, continued busily and happily to her eighty-ninth year.

[11] New York City Conveyances, Book 84 and 108.

3. Boyhood

Next to the mother's influence in the boy's life was that of nature. The scene of his birth in exile made such an indelible impression upon him that he always recalled the spot with pleasure, and years later, on a visit, he easily identified it though the house was gone. Little incidents connected with his life there faded away, but the picturesque views of the countryside and the location of the house on a little knoll with a beautiful green meadow spread out at its base and a fine clear brook gracefully winding through the grass, aroused in him an early love for the charms of nature. On returning to Tarrytown after the war, he saw for the first time his father's home, which to his boyish imagination was so large that it looked like a church without a steeple; and he remembered especially a fine spring, which gushed from the hill about thirty feet from the family residence.[12]

Tarrytown, which is situated in a beautiful region with secluded glens and well-wooded hills overlooking the lake-like Hudson, was, at the time of the Revolution, a small village and trading center with a dozen or more plain houses simply furnished. The points of principal interest were the old Dutch Church, where Dutch sermons were still preached, and the Phillips's Manor House, both built of stone nearly a century earlier and still standing; a tavern noted for its gossip as in other towns and celebrated in Paulding's tale, "Cobus Yerks"; one or two pioneer stores; a school house in Sleepy Hollow; a grain mill;

---

[12] Some years ago in paving the streets, the Tarrytown authorities caused the spring to be cemented over. A picture of the Paulding residence, a two-story frame house with probably eight rooms, is preserved in M. D. Raymond's *Souvenir of the Revolutionary Soldiers' Monument Dedication at Tarrytown, N. Y.* (1894).

and the dock at Paulding's house, from which a market boat made weekly trips to New York, then as far away as Boston is today. The good people in and around the hamlet, mostly Dutch farmers, were plain, industrious, and practical, a bit superstitious but not fanatical; faithful church-goers and inveterate foes of novelty. In the Dutch church records they clung loyally to the Dutch money system till 1745, and to sermons preached in Dutch till 1785, when Rev. Stephen Van Voorhees began to preach and keep the records in English, which even then offended some of the Dutch conservatives. During the Revolution the church was closed, and weddings and baptisms waited. Like most people in those days, the Tarrytown Dutch had few books, and local means for only an imperfect elementary education.[13]

During the Revolution they served the American cause loyally, though their landlord, Mr. Phillips, sided with the British and tried by intimidation to make them join him. In 1779 the people who remained in Tarrytown petitioned the New York Legislature for relief, stating that they were exposed to the ravages of the enemy, had repeatedly lost live stock, and been plundered of clothing, beds, beef, pork, and furniture; that their houses and barns had been burnt; and that many persons were either imprisoned or dead. But they received no substantial relief till the war ended. The British General Howe once paid them a fine compliment: "I can do nothing with this Dutch population; I can neither buy them with money nor conquer them with force."[14] And in 1780 the whole country rang with joy over the exploit of John Paulding, David Williams, and Isaac Van Wart in capturing Major André and thereby saving West Point. In such a region, echoing

[13] E. M. Bacon's *Chronicles of Tarrytown and Sleepy Hollow.*
[14] *Souvenir Rev. Sol. Mon. Dedication, Tarrytown,* pp. 23–24.

with tales of heroism and British depredations, James K.
Paulding grew up to the age of eighteen.

There was ample reason for the anti-British feeling exhibited in much of his early writing. For more than a
hundred years the Dutch had been subject to the British.
Paulding was conceived and born while his mother was a
refugee from her home because of British hostility; he
grew up in a region devastated by the invader and charged
with bitter feeling toward England. Nine men of the
Paulding family, including his father and three uncles,
had served in the American Army. His first cousin, John
Paulding, and his brother-in-law, Lieutenant Isaac Requa,
had experienced the horrors of British prisons in New
York. His maternal grandfather, Nathaniel Ogden, because he had refused to cry, "God save the King!" had been
cruelly cut across the head by a party of British soldiers,
and, in consequence, had become partially and permanently
deranged in mind. James remembered him as a pitiful,
white-haired old man, walking along the beach at Tarrytown, picking up sticks, talking to himself, and calling the
Tories highway robbers.

Paulding's opportunities for schooling were limited.
Under the old Dutch regime, an attempt had been made to
supply every community with a minister and a schoolmaster supported by the people; the aim was universal
education without sex discrimination. The royal English
governors, though they licensed Dutch teachers and preachers, had been somewhat disinclined to educate the whole
people; and under them almost the only constructive measure was the founding in 1754 of King's College (now
Columbia), which the governor mistakenly hoped would
prevent the further growth of republican principles. Even
the crude elementary schools that had previously existed
collapsed during the Revolution, and they revived slowly.

Though Governor George Clinton in 1782 urged the legislature to promote public education as the peculiar duty of a free government and declared that the war had caused a decline in education extremely injurious to the rising generation, yet no really effective system was established till 1812.[15]

"For some time after the conclusion of the war," wrote Paulding, "there were very few schools in our part of the country, and the nearest school-house was upward of two miles from our residence. At this country school, which was a log hut, I received my education." For convenience in attending, he lived with an uncle on a farm east of Tarrytown, and usually walked to school alone. At his uncle's the only companion of his own age was a dumb girl, the daughter of an improvident but witty old soldier who was allowed free quarters on the farm. The girl, forty years later, gave title to Paulding's pathetic tale, "The Dumb Girl." For parts of three or four years he attended this school, which stopped unceremoniously when the schoolmaster was appointed surrogate of the county. Thus ended the boy's formal schooling, which had cost about fifteen dollars. He then returned to his mother's home, a good-sized boy of twelve or thirteen years. Fortunately he had acquired a taste for reading. Among the few books owned by his uncle was a copy of Goldsmith's *The Citizen of the World*. It so fascinated the youth that he read it at least twenty times, and the author became his model of English prose. In his father's house there were also a few books saved from the wreck, and with these he fed his imagination. But the scarcity of books and magazines induced an excellent habit: "What I read I read thoroughly, and what I learned I learned well. A book was then a treasure."

[15] Sherman Williams' *New York's Part in History*, pp. 337–374.

The most remarkable feature, however, of his boyhood
is that he was unhappy. Observe his statements:

"From the experience of my early life I never wish to be
young again." . . . "My disposition was proud and shy. . . .
My life at Tarrytown after leaving school was weary and irksome. The present was a blank and the future almost a void.
My mind was sufficiently active, but my body indolent. . . .
There was never any employment for my idle hours. . . . I was
always fond of reading, but we had few books, and there was
no public library." . . . "I lived pretty much in a world of my
own creating."

While at school, he was dreamy and melancholy; he
became ill and was troubled by the fear of death. In
consequence of the excitement attending a revival and his
own temporary despondency, he was at one time nearly
demented. Since the Dutch were eminently cheerful, and
Paulding's own later life was distinguished for its good
cheer and serene humor, and for its rational ease and
composure, it appears that his mind had grown preco-
ciously and was secretly grappling with human problems
he was then unable to solve.

Near the beginning of this period of juvenile dejection,
reminding one of the boyhood of Poe or De Quincey, his
family apparently sought to divert him. His brother William gave him a gun; and James tried hunting and 'fishing.
In winter, he set traps and snares for small game. With
gun in hand, he explored the Tarrytown region, mysteriously associated with many a supernatural tale or
with incidents of the Revolution. On one occasion, proud
as a Roman conqueror, he came down Tarrytown hill with
five quails, a partridge, and a rabbit; at another time, the
dreaming boy, holding his gun carelessly, let it explode
accidentally so near his head as to tear a hole in the brim
of his hat. After this he decided to abandon hunting and

to become a fisherman. His greatest piscatory feat was
catching a bass twenty-two inches long. In time, he once
more heard joyfully the blue-jay chanting, the squirrel
chirping, and the pheasant drumming. The Tarrytown
landscape and people had also enchanted the youthful
Washington Irving; and it was here, probably about the
time when William Irving married James's sister, Julia
Paulding, that Washington Irving and James K. Paulding
became acquainted and collaborated in their sports as afterwards in their writings.[16]

In Paulding's tale entitled "Dyspepsy" and published
in 1829 there is an autobiographical introduction that casts
light on this unhappy period, revealing a thoughtful youth
with active imagination:

"Deprived thus of the resources of active employment, I spent
my time either in reading, or roaming at random and unpur-
posed, through the beautiful romantic scenes which surrounded
our poor, yet pleasant abode. . . . I was eternally thinking, and
doing nothing. The least spark awakened in my mind visions
of the future—for that was all to me—and lighted my path
through long perspectives of shadowy happiness. Sometimes I
was a soldier, winning my way to the highest heaven of military
glory; sometimes a poet, the admiration of the fair; and sometimes I possessed what then seemed to me the sure means of
perfect happiness—ten thousand a year. For days, and weeks,
and months, and years, I hardly spoke an unnecessary word,
and millions of thoughts, wishes, fears, and hopes, millions of
impulses and impressions arose in my mind and died away, without ever receiving a being through the medium of my tongue or
my pen. . . .

"I was always in love with some one; for love was indis-
pensable to my visionary existence. . . . But when I was in love,
I always ran away. I would as soon have met a spirit as the
object of my affections. . . . I grew up to the age of seventeen
or eighteen, a sheer, abstract man—a being of thought rather

[16] *Literary Life of James K. Paulding,* pp. 25–28.

than action. . . . Yet, for all this, I became neither mad nor an idiot. It seemed as if I was all this time preparing myself for realities; and that my sojournings in the world of fancy imperceptibly initiated me into the material world."

CHAPTER II

IN " THE GREAT COMMERCIAL EMPORIUM"

AN important event in Paulding's life was his removal
to the City of New York in 1796 or 1797, when he was about
eighteen years of age. From the village simplicity and
quiet of Tarrytown, he was introduced into the varied life
and activity of a rapidly growing city visited by many
travelers and sending its ships to all parts of the world.
He came with only seven dollars in his pocket, but his
brother William had got him a clerical position in a public
office, probably in the United States Loan Office. Hitherto,
though he had not traveled more than five miles from
home, he had heard rumors and dreamed dreams of the
city, which in his youth he pictured as the world of romance, ineffable wonders, wise men, and beautiful women,
but which in his maturity he christened more accurately
"The Great Commercial Emporium."

According to his own frank statement, the first shock to
his shy, sensitive nature was the jeer he received from the
rabble about the wharf for walking in the middle of the
street; but at the hospitable and jovial home of William
Irving, the eldest brother of Washington, he was affection-
ately welcomed by his sister, Julia Irving, and her husband, and his own brother William, the lawyer. The location, at 43 Vesey Street, was pleasant. From the Irving
house he could look north over the campus of Columbia
College, west over a green slope to the Hudson River, and
east to St. Paul's Chapel, Broadway, and the public build-

19

ings. James lived here until about 1806, when he accompanied the Irving family to 287 Greenwich Street, north of Columbia College.[1]

The fatherly interest of William Irving (1766–1821) in his brother-in-law, James K. Paulding, as well as in Washington Irving, deserves a warm tribute. William Irving was a versatile, large-hearted gentleman. He could not accept the strict Scotch beliefs of his father, but he ultimately became a sincere Episcopalian, influencing James in that direction. As a young man, he had conducted for four years a profitable fur trade with the Indians of the Mohawk Valley, and on his trips there had stopped long enough at Tarrytown to win the heart of Julia Paulding, who doubtless inherited some of her mother's virtues and practiced them in her home. Returning to New York, he engaged in the mercantile business and later in politics, with literature and banking as avocations. He was three times chosen congressman by the Democrats, resigning in April, 1818, because of failing health; in the War of 1812, he strongly advocated national conscription to raise an army of 80,000 men for two years. He was a mellow humorist, anecdotal, sensitive, and appreciative. James K. Paulding praised him as "a man of great wit, genius, and originality"; and his brother Washington wrote, "He was the man I most loved on earth." Living in intimate association with such a man for many years meant great intellectual and spiritual growth for Paulding, who was also happily placed to form the most desirable friendships, especially with members of the Calliopean society. Many of his problems were solved; the clouds of gloom and despondency that had shadowed his boyhood slowly faded

[1] *Literary Life*, pp. 29 and 283; Paulding's story, "Dyspepsy"; "Literary Landmarks of New York" in *The Critic*, Vol. 42, pp. 53–58 (Jan., 1903).

away, and he became happy and contented; life took on roseate hues; and his taste for humor, literature, and politics grew apace.[2]

James K. Paulding may have come too late to join a literary society, called the Calliopean, which a group of young men ambitious for self-cultivation had organized in 1788, and which by 1791 had thirty-three members, including William and Peter Irving and William Paulding. This society, which preceded the famous Salmagundi group, was active and well organized; its by-laws imposed fines for neglect of duty and unbecoming conduct at the meetings, and its founding was annually celebrated as an important event. The members met every week for practice in debate, oratory, and composition; they recited passages from Addison's *Cato*, Pope's poems, and Shakespeare's plays; they bought books; and they wrote original prose and verse. Among the topics for debate were the freedom of the will, the value of theaters, and the wisdom of increasing the territory of the United States. William Paulding became a leading orator, and Peter Irving used to entertain the young literati with parodies, as for example one on "To be or not to be." They kept a bound record of their sessions, two volumes of which are extant and available in the library of the New York Historical Society. Since the second volume ends with March, 1795, it is not known when the society was discontinued or whether James K. Paulding became a member, though he was certainly influenced by the literary impulse it created and fostered.

His brother, William Paulding (1770–1854), who joined the Calliopean in 1789 and was studying law in 1795, became a capable attorney and successful politician. Though

---

2 *A Biographical Congressional Directory, 1774–1911* (Washington, 1913); P. M. Irving's *Life and Letters of Washington Irving; National Intelligencer* (Washington, D. C.), January 3, 1815.

he was an effective speaker, as James was an effective writer, yet there is no evidence that they attracted each other especially.   By 1811 William had accumulated sufficient wealth to own a country seat, and sufficient prominence to win a Democratic seat in Congress.   He was a brigadier general in the War of 1812, and a delegate to the state constitutional convention of 1821; excepting one year, he was mayor of New York from 1823 to 1827, and in August, 1824, welcomed the venerable Lafayette to the city.   In 1829 he presided in an able and impartial manner over the convention for revising and amending the city charter.   At one time he was considered for governor. About 1840 he built by the Hudson River below Tarrytown the palatial stone castle now owned by Helen Gould Shepard.   His portrait, painted in 1826 by Samuel F. B. Morse and hanging in the New York City Hall, presents a serious, judicial face with strong chin, prominent nose, thin lips, and brown eyes.   His counterpart in the Irving family was the very successful Judge John T. Irving, for twenty years a trustee of Columbia College.   From the two Williams and John T. Irving, Paulding could easily get ample inside information for satirizing politicians.

More important still, the boyish acquaintance between James K. Paulding and Washington Irving was renewed and ripened into an enduring friendship.   Though Paulding was more than four and a half years older, they had many traits in common.   Both kept away from college; both were fond of the theater; both had literary tastes to gratify; both had fertile imaginations; secretly perhaps, each was ambitious to write.   Washington, as is well known, stole away from home, in violation of his father's interdict against the theater, to join James in seeing Joseph Jefferson, the comedian, play Jack Arable's part in Reynolds's "Speculation."   Perhaps, they saw in 1797 a

WILLIAM PAULDING (1770–1854)

Mayor of New York and Congressman, and the Oldest Brother of
J. K. Paulding

Reproduced from a copy of the portrait made by Samuel F. B. Morse,
inventor of the telegraph.

farce entitled "Doldrum," the story of a man who slept
from 1796 to 1803, which may have influenced the plot
of "Rip Van Winkle." [3]   Their friendship continued
throughout life, but was more intimate before Irving's
long absence abroad than afterwards.   It resembled the
literary friendship between Wordsworth and Coleridge,
in that Irving's good fellowship and romantic fancy stimulated the meditative Paulding much as Coleridge's rich
talk and glowing imagination cheered and drew out the
genius of Wordsworth.

With these happy personal associations and others
formed later, young Paulding was in a position to profit
most from city life.

"In great cities," he wrote some years later, "the hours of re-
laxation may be spent in various amusements, innocent, and
even elegant in their nature.   Nay, there is something in the
very aspect of a large town, in the perpetual succession of
objects novel and various, that present continual amusements
to the mind, without the trouble of seeking it laboriously or ex-
pensively." [4]

The New York of 1800 or thereabouts was very different
from the modern steel-ribbed, sky-scraping metropolis.   A
somewhat informal, easy-mannered spirit of good fellowship prevailed.   A traveler entering the city from the
ocean would observe first of all the church spires and then
a forest of tall masts with white sails of the many ships
anchored in the East River.   Approaching nearer, he
would notice that the houses were usually of red brick with
tiled roofs and only two or three stories high; among these,
an occasional Dutch house with crow-stepped gable end

[3] George O. Seilhamer's *History of the American Theatre*, pp. 384
and 397 (Philadelphia, 1891).
[4] *Letters from the South*, Vol. 1, p. 70.

facing the street. At the wharf, he would hear the rumble
of some of the thousand cartmen's wagons handling the
city's merchandise. Ashore, he would find William Street
a shopping center, and poplar-shaded Broadway between
the Battery and the city buildings the principal prom-
enade, faced by handsome residences and attractive shops.
In the afternoons comely dames and gay daughters, little
rouged but tight-laced, would search the shops for bits
of French finery. Our traveler would discover a prosperous, progressive city, extending about two miles from
the Battery, with a mixed population of 60,000, which had
nearly doubled in the preceding decade. Here and there
he would see traces of the fire that during the Revolution
had destroyed about one-third of the city, and he would
hear shocking stories of the British occupation. At the
hundred taverns, hotels, and coffee houses there would be
a host of politicians, brokers, merchants, and travelers,
chatting, trafficking, animatedly discussing Jefferson's pol-
icies, or Napoleon's ambitions, or city extensions, or reading the numerous little newspapers then cackling and hoot-
ing around the country.

About the public buildings are half a hundred well-fed
lawyers, including Alexander Hamilton, Aaron Burr, and
De Witt Clinton. Somewhere in the city are about twice
that number of indigent, miscellaneous teachers, many of
them foreign tutors in rich families. The thirty or forty
bookstores of all kinds carry a few native productions such
as Jefferson's *Notes on Virginia* and C. B. Brown's novels,
but ample stocks of law books, histories, travels, Bibles,
eighteenth-century English authors, magazines, and some
sentimental or supernatural fiction for the ladies. Our
traveler would find William Dunlap in charge of the Park
Theater, employing a dozen actors and actresses and sup-
plying the town with Shakespeare's masterpieces, Kotze-

bue's German plays, and theatrical gossip. From the number of ships and stores and night business schools, he is easily convinced that the city holds seven or eight hundred merchants. There is not a single steamboat builder or automobile manufacturer, but a dozen or more coachmakers and a score or two of sail-makers, besides a few dentists, engravers, portrait painters, and manufacturers. North of the city limits, where the numbered cross streets now run, he would discover a well-kept countryside with meadows and fields, orchards and gardens, reminiscent of Holland; the sites of Madison Square and Columbus Circle would be rural, and Harlem is an insignificant town eight or ten miles away.[5]

Concerning his early experiences in New York Paulding later said:

"Thus I fell, as it were, among the Philistines; for the circle in which I moved—though I can scarcely say had a being—was composed of young men, many of whom have since made no inconsiderable figure in the world. I was excessively thin-skinned—I may say, perfectly raw—and nothing was so painful to me as ridicule. They broke me in by quizzing me most unmercifully; but, though the perspiration of almost agony sprung from the very hair of my head, I bore it like a martyr, for I was too proud to show how I suffered. By this course I was drilled into something like a citizen of the new world into which I had been thrown. It was a rough discipline to a lad of my temperament, but proved of great service in after-life. It was the best school in which I ever studied." [6]

[5] N. Y. City Directories from 1786 to 1805; paintings of the city from different points of view; details gleaned from Washington Irving's Letters, J. W. Francis' *Old New York*, John Davis' *Travels of Four Years and a Half in the United States of America* (1798–1802), John Lambert's *Travels Through Lower Canada and the United States* (1806–1808), O. S. Coad's *William Dunlap*, contemporary newspapers, etc.

[6] *Literary Life*, pp. 29–30.

Of this formative period of Paulding's life few intimate details have been preserved. During the day he was busy at his clerical position; in the evening he would chat with his friends, or attend the theater with some of the Irvings; more likely he would sit quietly at home, reading an English magazine, or books borrowed from his friends or loaned by the New York Society Library, which then had a collection of 6000 volumes, or by some of the bookstores, which conducted circulating departments. It seems that he also studied music and French. With William Irving he would sometimes engage in wit combats, especially over the rival claims of England and France to a place in the sun, with Paulding warmly defending his Frenchmen and seeking by an appeal to history to establish his points. On Sundays he would hear some of the city's leading preachers, among whom was Dr. John M. Mason, a powerful epigrammatic speaker but too dogmatical to please Paulding; or, like Wordsworth, he would seek communion with the Creator in the solitudes of nature. At times he would be persuaded by Washington Irving to take walks about the town and country or to pay their respects to the young ladies. In contrast with the idle dreaming of his boyhood, he enjoyed ample physical and mental employment.

In the commercial emporium Paulding lived till 1845, with the exception of eleven years when he was an official in Washington. The City of New York with its people, libraries, churches, theaters, bookstores, newspapers, and commercial activities became his training school, his university; there he was principally educated. Like Irving, he apparently had no ambition to attend Columbia College; besides, he could not have passed the entrance examinations in Latin and Greek, and the rule of 1810, if previously in force, dismissing any student who during the months of study should attend a public amusement, would have been sufficent to keep him away.[7] Like Franklin and Whitman, Paulding worked out his own scholastic salvation; and in due time, the shy, unsophisticated boy with undisciplined imagination became an efficient naval official, a well-read man, a competent critic, and a popular novelist with an international reputation.

Though Paulding before 1800 wrote verses imitative of Gray and Pope, and scribbled in commonplace books, he first attained the distinction of print in a newspaper venture conducted by Peter Irving (1772–1838), an elder brother of Washington's. Diverted from the study of law by his father, who regarded it as hardly an honest calling, Peter had taken a degree in medicine from Columbia in 1794, but, finding the profession uncongenial, he abandoned it, though the title "Doctor" remained for life. With a taste for the fine arts, he soon afterwards joined a group of dramatic censors, who endeavored to improve the local theater by giving it intelligent criticism in the newspapers. He was also prominent in secret and literary societies and local military organizations. In 1802 he established and published for three or four years a four-page daily newspaper, *The Morning Chronicle,* one of the half-dozen papers then issued in New York. Its announced purpose was to support the present administration, to establish a useful business paper, to blend literature with commerce and politics, and to support a liberal Christian system. The price was eight dollars a year. In this dignified sheet, Paulding's writings, probably in the form of letters, editorials, and news items published anonymously, first achieved print. Peter was a courteous, refined gentleman, and wrote with some charm, but after 1809 his long residence of twenty-seven years in Europe

[7] *History of Columbia University, 1754–1904,* pp. 91–92.

and his invalidism prevented his playing a more active part in the early development of New York culture.[8]

The absence of Washington Irving in Europe from May, 1804 to March, 1806 on account of ill health opened a correspondence between him and Paulding. James missed the witty, animated conversation of his friend, for whom, according to William Irving, the grand desideratum was good company. In June, James wrote to him, closing with this self-revealing passage:

"You will hear by this same conveyance of the welfare of all your friends—of them I shall therefore say nothing. But for my 'single self' I tender the best good wishes of my heart for your health and happiness. I have been called cold-hearted, and indifferent to the welfare of others, because my manners are perhaps so. But it was injustice, and among the many wishes you may receive be assured there will be none more sincere or more earnest than mine." [9]

Informally imitating the Calliopean society, Irving had already assembled a group of nicknamed friends, with an inner circle consisting of himself, Henry Brevoort Jr. ("Nuncle"), Gouverneur Kemble ("The Patroon"), and James K. Paulding ("Billy Taylor"). Of these Henry Brevoort (1782–1848) was the most intimate with Irving; he was prospectively rich by inheritance from the landed estate of his Dutch father; he was amiable, generous, magnanimous; a patron of the fine arts. Abroad, he met Scott and gave him a copy of Irving's Knickerbocker History; with his wife, who was a southern lady, and their children, he spent several years in Europe. From his correspondence with Irving it is reasonable to suppose that but for his wealth and indolence he might have

---

[8] *The Morning Chronicle* (1802–1806); *Life and Letters of Washington Irving.*

[9] *Literary Life,* p. 34.

succeeded in literature. Paulding's preference after Irving was probably Gouverneur Kemble, brother of Gertrude Kemble, who later became Paulding's wife. Kemble graduated from Columbia in 1803; after traveling abroad, he dabbled in politics, going to Congress in 1838, and settled down to business,—railroads and manufactures; he was a wholesome, cultivated man, and outlived his friends. His house at Cold Spring was a favorite haunt of authors and politicians. A very popular member of the group was Henry Ogden ("Super-cargo"), a cheerful, light-hearted fellow. Other members of Irving's "Lads of Kilkenny" were David Porter ("Sinbad"), Ebenezer Irving ("Captain Greatheart"), Peter Irving ("The Doctor"), Richard McCall (Oorombates"), and a few others. The favorite city resort of the nine worthies was Dyde's genteel public house in Park Row near the theater; for week-ends, especially in the summer, they preferred an old family mansion with antique furniture owned by Gouverneur Kemble and situated on the bank of the Passaic above Newark, New Jersey. This was a kind of fraternity house, and the scene of many juvenile pranks and frolics; in *Salmagundi* it is known as Cockloft Hall. The members of the inner circle sometimes made longer excursions to the hospitable seat of Captain Phillipse in the Highlands. Of those days the Salmagundi punch bowl, which is preserved by the New York Historical Society, and the Salmagundi periodical are the best mementos.[10]

[10] George S. Hellman's Introduction to *Letters of Henry Brevoort to Washington Irving; Literary Life of James K. Paulding*, pp. 35–38; P. M. Irving's *Life and Letters of Washington Irving*.

CHAPTER III

SALMAGUNDI AND OTHER LITERARY EXPERIMENTS

IN the annals of the United States few years are more noteworthy than 1807. In that year Congress recognized the development of a strong anti-slavery sentiment by prohibiting the importation of African slaves; and the new republic safely weathered the seditious movement headed by Aaron Burr, whose arrest culminated in a spectacular trial at Richmond, Virginia. The romantic Robert Fulton, fresh from foreign travels, revolutionized water traffic by perfecting the steamboat; and the embargo act encouraged American manufacturing. In literature, a group of youthful New York wits broke with the tradition of formal prose and won a notable success in the Salmagundi papers. Just as the *Lyrical Ballads* of 1798 marked a new era in English poetry, so did the *Salmagundi* of 1807 mark the beginning of a simpler fashion in American prose.

On January 24, 1807, up-to-date New Yorkers found themselves eagerly buying and discussing a little, yellow-backed, thirty-page pamphlet that could be easily carried in a man's coat pocket or in a lady's purse. It bore the whimsical title, *Salmagundi; or, The Whim-Whams and Opinions of Launcelot Langstaff, Esq. and Others.* Beneath the name there was a fantastic quotation, mocking the English literary practice of quoting choice bits of Latin as mottoes, and striking the keynote of the periodical. In the introductory article the unnamed authors jocularly announced their purpose "to instruct the young,

30

reform the old, correct the town, and castigate the age;
this is an arduous task, and therefore we undertake it
with confidence. We intend for this purpose to present
a striking picture of the town; and as everybody is anxious
to see his own phiz on canvas, however stupid or ugly
it may be, we have no doubt but the whole town will flock
to our exhibition.'' Both the authors and the publisher
professed a sublime contempt for the pecuniary success of
the paper, which would appear at irregular intervals to
suit the convenience of the authors; as laughing philosophers, they were eager to entertain their readers and to
conceal themselves behind pseudonyms. The first number
ended effectively with humorous accounts of recent New
York theatrical performances and dancing assemblies.
The second, dated February 4, continued the wit of the
first, and introduced the humorous bachelor, Pindar Cockloft, who made rhymes on the follies of the new fashions.
In the third there appeared the first of nine serial letters
on New York attributed to a fictitious Tripolitan named
Mustapha Rub-a-Dub Keli Khan, recently a prisoner in
the city. Thereafter, the principal topics were the Cockloft family, English travelers in America, fashions,
theaters, descriptions of nature, character sketches, Pindar
Cockloft's verses, a chapter on the ancient city of Gotham,
and other miscellanies. Since number twenty, the last,
was published on January 25, 1808, the pamphlets on an
average appeared every two or three weeks.

Audacious and spiced with wit, *Salmagundi* became an
immediate success. Cleverly advertised and expectantly
awaited, many of the separate numbers passed through
several editions; a bound copy in a Boston library contains individual numbers in the fourth and fifth editions.
With each number the public interest increased; 800 copies
at a shilling apiece were sold in a day—a record for that

time. Its fame extended to other cities; the authors were astonished at the success of their venture. The publisher, David Longworth, secured a copyright, and before it expired in 1822, Paulding estimated that the sales amounted to ten or fifteen thousand dollars. Paulding and Irving, however, received only one hundred dollars apiece, and the publication was abruptly discontinued, because the authors and the publisher could not amicably adjust their sublime contempt for the financial gains. John Lambert, an Englishman, who was then in New York and who edited the London edition of 1811, states in his excellent preface that the numbers received "unprecedented applause and passed through several editions during the course of their publication." Since Longworth issued the second American edition in 1814 and the third in 1820, it is evident that *Salmagundi* could subsist without the aid of Irving's later masterpieces. Altogether, down to 1902, it had attained at least thirty-four editions—nineteen American, thirteen English, one French, and one Swedish. Of these, the English with one exception appeared in the first half of the century, indicating lively British curiosity about American affairs; and most of the American editions appeared in the second half of the century, indicating a native revival of interest in early New York. On an average, then, *Salmagundi*, either in separate or in collected editions, has been republished every three years since it first greeted New Yorkers.

This novel periodical elicited some noteworthy contemporary comments both abroad and at home. In England, John Lambert, characterizing it as "a dish of real American cookery," stated: "The distinguishing feature of the Salmagundian Essays is humorous satire, which runs through the whole work like veins of rich ore in the bowels of the earth. These essays partake more of the broad humour and satirical wit of Rabelais and Swift than the refined morality of Addison and Johnson; their chief aim is to raise a laugh at the expense of folly and absurdity.''[1] In a friendly critique *The Monthly Review* of London welcomed *Salmagundi* as a commendable specimen of American literature, praised the descriptions and character sketches, and granted that the authors ''certainly excel in an adroit species of irony.''[2]   Still more significant are the opinion and prediction of Sir Walter Scott, recorded in a letter to Washington Irving, dated December 4, 1819: ''Knickerbocker and Salmagundi are more exclusively American [than *The Sketch-Book*], and may not be quite so well suited for our meridian.   But they are so excellent in their way, that if the public attention could be once turned on them I am confident that they would become popular.''[3]   At home, the *North American Review*, while praising the early numbers of *The Sketch-Book*, reverted to *Salmagundi*, stated that its fortunate appearance in New York prevented its being looked out of countenance and talked down by supercilious people, and acknowledged that it was ''the ablest work of wit and humour which we had produced.''[4]

These disinterested commendations, verified by time, are best explained by the fact that *Salmagundi* was written by three wits and published by a fourth.   The authorship was so well concealed that John Lambert could hear only whispers of a lawyer and two merchants, and even as late as March, 1832, the editor of the *New York Mirror* after careful enquiry felt the need of publishing an authentic

[1] Introductory Essay to London edition of 1811.

[2] Vol. 65, pp. 418–424, August, 1811.

[3] P. M. Irving's *Life and Letters of Washington Irving*, Vol. 1, p. 444.

[4] Vol. 9, p. 334, September, 1819.

statement, assigning all the poetry and two of the prose
articles to William Irving and the rest in about equal but
unidentified parts to Washington Irving and James K.
Paulding.[5]   Of course, in literary circles the Irving-
Paulding combination was previously known.   For some
years the authors had been intermittently writing for the
newspapers.   Washington Irving at twenty-four had
recently returned from a two-year trip to Europe, had
passed the bar examination, and was popular in New York
and Philadelphia society; Paulding, past twenty-eight, was
a handsome young man, alert and satirical.   Between them
Salmagundi arose.   P. M. Irving states that Washington
proposed the plan of the publication to Paulding, who
readily fell in with it, wrote his part, and was in full
charge when Irving went to Burr's trial in Richmond.
Later, they were joined by William Irving, who completed
the trio of wits and wrote the verse.

To determine the authorship of the separate Salmagundi
papers is a knotty problem.   They have always been published together, and no author ever fully indicated his
share.   In fact, Paulding stated in the Harper edition of
his works (1835) that the essays were so literally joint
productions that it would be difficult to assign to each his
exact part.   P. M. Irving, however, upon the authority of
the chief writers, credits the six poems and two of the
Mustapha letters (in Nos. 5 and 14) to William Irving,
and assigns the rest of the essays, a few specifically, to
Washington Irving and to Paulding, with the statement
that Paulding's share in the work, though it could not be
accurately discriminated, was equal to Washington Irving's.[6]   He credits Paulding with beginning and writing

<hr />

[5] *New York Mirror,* Vol. 9, p. 295.

[6] P. M. Irving's *Life and Letters of Washington Irving,* Vol. 1,
p. 178.

(in Nos. 3 and 18) two of the Mustapha letters, which as a whole became very popular and were probably suggested by Goldsmith's *The Citizen of the World;* to Paulding he also assigns the Langstaff article in No. 1, the second and third in No. 2, "Mine Uncle John" in No. 11, and the New Year essay in No. 20. In addition, it is highly probable from internal evidences of style and theme that Paulding wrote the prose sketches of the Cockloft family in Nos. 6, 9, 12, and 14, and the essays "On Style," "A Retrospect," "On Greatness," "Style at Ballston," and "Autumnal Reflections." In the composition of the character sketches, especially the sketch of Aunt Charity (No. 9), Irving may have participated.

To its eccentric publisher, David Longworth, who was also a bookdealer, collector of plays, and exhibitor of paintings, proper credit is due. He used to gratify his taste and reduce his bank account by publishing handsome literary collections, but he would reimburse himself as proprietor of the New York City directory. In him business sense and literary taste mingled in the right proportions to make a successful advertiser; his book shop in Park Row near the theater he called the Shakespeare Gallery in honor of Boydell's engravings on exhibition there, and of a huge painting, on the front of his shop, of the crowning of Shakespeare. In the directory for 1804, he ran a witty advertisement, declaring that he was determined to be silent about his business and to let people discover it for themselves. The next year he versified his accomplishments, thus celebrating the directory:

> "The people liked it wondrous well,
>   Both high and low degree,
>   For there each one, in black and white,
>   His own dear name might see.

> "It told his neighbor's dwelling place
> To each enquiring elf;
> And, what was more important still,
> Told where he lived himself.

*   *   *   *

> "This song the minstrel often sung,
> Which did his hearers please,
> And though it brought him little fame,
> It brought him bread and cheese."

It is significant that in Evergreen's account of Langstaff (No. 8) and "Sketches from Nature" (No. 15), Washington Irving chose Paulding for his subject. Though Irving allowed his imagination and humor to play with the facts, he drew a substantially true sketch of his friend, characterizing him as "rich in many of the sterling qualities of our nature," gifted with a vivacious and satirical fancy, and viewing the world as a solitary spectator. "And trust me, gentle folk," Irving concludes, "his are the whim-whams of a courteous gentleman full of most excellent qualities; honourable in his disposition, independent in his sentiments, and of unbounded good nature, as may be seen through all his works." In "Sketches from Nature," Irving pictures Paulding (Langstaff) dreaming and discoursing by a riverside. The essay is Irving's recognition of Paulding's rooted love of nature, a love somewhat melancholy then but becoming joyful. In Paulding he sees a thinker, who had written beautifully of his observations of nature.

But *Salmagundi* will never be a classic. "The work," Irving wrote to Brevoort in 1819, "was pardonable as a juvenile production, but it is full of errors, puerilities, and imperfections. I was in hopes it would gradually have gone down into oblivion,"—an opinion that P. M. Irving justly called rigorous and oversensitive. In 1824, Paulding came nearer the truth in a letter to his friend: "I don't hold this early bantling of ours in such utter contempt as you do, and can't help viewing it in the light of a careless popular thing that will always be read in spite of its faults, perhaps in consequence of these very faults." The modern reader may wonder how it could excite so much interest a century ago; certainly its satires on the dandies and follies of 1807 have little appeal nowadays. Indeed, excepting the Mustapha letters and two or three character sketches, the first volume is hardly more than good modern journalism. The authors, however, improved by practice, and, having captivated the town with the witty audacity of the early numbers and acquired greater confidence in their own powers, showed both humor and sense in the second volume. Here are the character sketches of "Mine Uncle John" and "The Little Man in Black," true predecessors of Paulding's "Cobus Yerks" and Irving's "The Stout Gentleman"; here are pleasant descriptions of nature; here we find Paulding affirming that there are two kinds of greatness—"one conferred by heaven—the exalted nobility of the soul;—the other, a spurious distinction, engendered by the mob and lavished upon its favourites." Here we discover Irving's humorous chapter upon the ancient city of Gotham, and here, too, Mustapha's eloquent letter on fame in Irving's best manner, concluding,

"Alas! alas! said I to myself, how mutable are the foundations on which our proudest hopes of future fame are reposed! He who imagines he has secured to himself the meed of deathless renown, indulges in deluding visions, which only bespeak the vanity of the dreamer. The storied obelisk—the triumphant arch,—the swelling dome, shall crumble into dust, and the names they would preserve from oblivion shall often pass away, before their own duration is accomplished."

The writers owed something to Steele, Addison, and

Goldsmith, to Swift and Rabelais; but much more to their own vivacity and native wit, to their determination to write entertainingly and let their intelligence play over the panorama around them, to their relish for eccentric characters, to their dislike of the pompous prose style then fashionable in America, and to the practice of using the language of real men though it should be abrupt and slangy. Irving and Paulding even then had individual styles, though less well marked than later: the former was romantic, humorous, courteous, and vivacious; the latter, realistic, satirical, civil, and jocose. They reflected the gayety, prosperity, sanity, and liberality of New York.

Salmagundi, however, should be contrasted, not compared, with *The Spectator,* because *The Spectator* was composed by mature, experienced authors, scholarly, refined, and wise, and it was their masterpiece. *Salmagundi,* on the other hand, was the spontaneous creation of two youthful writers, whose strength lay, not in deep, rich thought, nor in a 'finished style, but in their vivacity, good humor, originality, and wish to entertain. *The Spectator* may be likened to a sprightly widow of thirty-five, sophisticated, dignified, yet, like the Mona Lisa, captivating all eyes and winning a train of admirers. But *Salmagundi* resembles an American girl of sixteen, light-hearted, rejoicing in health, witty and self-reliant, smiling infectiously, shocking her maiden aunts yet doing no wrong.

The success of *Salmagundi* stimulated the literary ambitions of the authors. Like prospectors in a new land, they had discovered literary gold, and though the title of the first venture passed to the publisher through their indifference, they were encouraged to undertake other literary adventures, which ultimately attracted international attention. In 1809, Irving, writing in the humorously exaggerated style of the Mustapha letters, published his comical history of the New York Dutch; and ten years later, when he was dejected by financial disasters, the memory of the Salmagundi and Knickerbocker success helped him to decide, in the face of family opposition, to enter the literary profession resolutely and wholeheartedly. Paulding, thereafter, writing alone and developing slowly yet steadily and surely, continued his literary experiments, sometimes succeeding, sometimes failing, but ultimately winning distinction and praise on both sides of the Atlantic. Down to 1820, he wrote six separate books in prose and verse, surpassing Irving in quantity by four volumes but falling decidedly behind him in quality. The merit of Irving's *The Sketch-Book* (1819-20) Paulding did not approach until he wrote ten years later his tales and novels of the New York Dutch. This delay was due partly to his political activities, partly to his engaging in the literary war against England, and partly to a hasty use of inferior literary matter. Meanwhile, Irving searched Europe and America for rich material to nourish his humor and imagination.

Of the period from 1808 to 1812 in Paulding's life we know little. It lies between the conclusion of *Salmagundi* and the publication of his first independent work. He was still supporting himself, probably writing for the newspapers, and penning verses in imitation of Milton's "L'Allegro." In 1809, we get a glimpse of him reading the Knickerbocker History. In November, 1810, he may have seen the actor, George Frederick Cooke, appear in Richard III and captivate the town so long as he remained sober. In the summer of 1812, Paulding proposed a second joint work to Irving, who agreed to it, but nothing came of the suggestion. In December, Paulding visited Washington, D. C.

Earlier in the same year, following Irving's success in

humorous history and probably taking a few hints from Francis Hopkinson's *A Pretty Story* (1774) or Jeremy Belknap's *The Foresters* (1792), he wrote and published the first of his John Bull satires. In *The Diverting History of John Bull and Brother Jonathan* (Philadelphia, 1812), Paulding came near striking off a little masterpiece of political satire. Falling short of this, the story was yet of sufficient merit and international interest to be republished the next year in London with favorable comments on its quaint humor and lively portrayal of character. A third edition appeared in Philadelphia in 1827, and eight years later in his collected works the author revised the original and added several brief chapters on the recent English travelers in America. The story was last published inauspiciously in 1867.

The original edition, an insignificant little book of 135 pages (18mo), divided into sixteen short chapters, sets forth, in the manner of *Gulliver's Travels,* the settlement and growth of the English colonies in America, and the development through revolt and severance of an independent nation. For humorous effect, the setting is so minimized that the Atlantic Ocean becomes a millpond; England, a little island in it; the thirteen colonies, thirteen prosperous farms. In like manner, the participants are reduced to represent a family and its neighbors, and the American Revolution becomes a boxing bout between father Bull and son Jonathan. Literally, then, the narrative records the ups and downs of a family, whose members, John Bull and Mrs. Bull, their youngest son Jonathan and Mrs. Jonathan, are well-marked characters. Their differences are aggravated by an active and troublesome neighbor (Napoleon), called Beau Napperty.

This good-natured but unpolished satire shows unmistakably that Paulding was keenly interested in the politi-

cal developments that immediately preceded and followed
the American Revolution, and that the facts were so
familiar to him that he could play with them in a politico-
satirical allegory.   While the narrative is sometimes inconsistent and is deficient in detailed structure, yet it is
fairly well sustained and scarcely ever marred by digres-
sions.   The author had a sharp eye both for national and
sectional idiosyncrasies and follies, and for sane action
and sound common sense.   Fickle and perverse Mrs. Bull
and fickle and perverse Mrs. Jonathan represent, respec-
tively and appropriately, the English Parliament and the
American Congress, which are even now diverting.   The
author's style, though humorously countrified and unpolished, at its best somewhat resembles that of Swift in
racy simplicity and directness.

The satire begins in this fashion (edition of 1835) :

"John Bull was a choleric old fellow, who held a good manor
in the middle of a great millpond, and which, by reason of its
being quite surrounded by water, was generally called *Bullock
Island.*   Bull was an ingenious man, an exceeding good black-
smith, a dexterous cutler, and a notable weaver and pot-baker
besides.   He also brewed capital porter, ale, and small beer,
and was, in fact, a sort of jack of all trades, and good bottle-
companion, and passably honest as times go.

"But what tarnished all these qualities was a devilish quarrel-
some, overbearing disposition, which was always getting him
into some scrape or other.   The truth is, he never heard of a
quarrel going on among his neighbours, but his fingers itched to
be in the thickest of them; so that he was hardly ever seen
without a broken head, a black eye, or a bloody nose.   Such
was Squire Bull, as he was commonly called by the country
people his neighbours—one of those odd, testy, grumbling, boast-
ing old codgers, that never get credit for what they are, because
they are always pretending to be what they are not."

Mrs. Jonathan, representing the American Congress, is
thus depicted :

"The honest truth of the matter is, that she was one of the most whimsical, cross-grained, contradictory, and bedevilled termagants, that ever fell to the lot of mortal man. Though composed of but one body, she had as many minds as she could hold, and was almost always of at least *seventeen* different opinions. Her face had all the appearance of one of your patchwork coverlets, and the different parts seemed to be collected from all quarters of the globe. She had an eastern squint of the eye, a northern aspect, and a southern *complexion*. Then her language resembled the confusion of Babel; at one time she talked like a Frogmorean, at another like Bull's wife herself; sometimes she talked half French half English, and very rarely she talked like Brother Jonathan's wife."

Paulding's representation of New England's opposition to the War of 1812 and of her threatened secession, as well as certain reflections on New York's lethargy in contributing funds for the war, elicited a commentary and reply in the same year entitled *The Beauties of Brother Bull-Us by his loving Sister Bull-A* (New York). The anonymous author points out certain coarse phraseology and sentiments, and endeavors to clear New England from Paulding's discreditable imputations, which, however, were true. One of the author's statements indicates that 2000 copies of Paulding's satire were published.

Among his experiments in this decade were two volumes of verse, which will be referred to in Chapter VII. The first, a poem in five cantos entitled *The Lay of the Scottish Fiddle* and written to parody Walter Scott's verse stories, was published at Philadelphia in 1813, and the next year in London. Its descriptions and humor have some merit, but the story is obscure and uninteresting. The second, which was named *The Backwoodsman* and published in 1818, was more carefully wrought, but it failed to enhance the author's reputation. He also wrote the first draft of a play (See Chapter VI). He had not yet learned to tell a story effectively either in prose or in verse, and, unlike Cooper, he had no intimate knowledge of frontier life.

Early in 1813, Paulding upon Irving's invitation became a contributor to *The Analectic Magazine*, a monthly miscellany consisting of reprinted British articles and contributions from native authors, published in Philadelphia by Moses Thomas. After two years, Irving resigned the editorship, but Paulding wrote for it regularly until the end of 1816. Fifteen of his thirty articles were sketches of the naval commanders in the War of 1812 and accounts of the naval controversies that followed. Bryant in his discourse on Washington Irving stated that these sketches, accompanied by portraits, were a popular feature of the magazine. Like a safety valve, they allowed Paulding's patriotism and rising anti-British feeling to escape harmlessly. They also contain some valuable historical data. Having only meager knowledge of some of the commanders, however, the author fell into the unfortunate habit of padding his sketches with rhetorical phrases and patriotic sentiments, which led Irving to wish that his friend would divorce himself from the magazine.[7] Probably the best are the accounts of "John Paul Jones" and "The Navy," in which the author advocated a strong American fleet.

The remaining articles are less ephemeral. In a review of Charles Phillips' *The Emerald Isle,* Paulding likened the then fashionable narrative poem with long explanatory notes to "that multifarious variety of broken chairs, ancient bureaus, wornout tables, and other precious remains of antiquity, which every good housewife thinks it necessary to scour up, and carry along with her in her periodical migrations." In "The Idea of a True Patriot," an ironical essay, which Halleck admired and praised,[8] he satirized

[7] *Letters of Washington Irving to Henry Brevoort,* Vol. I, p. 174.
[8] *Putnam's Magazine* for February, 1868, Vol. 11, p. 238.

those false patriots who would sacrifice private virtue and seek only their own profit, reminding the reader of Samuel Johnson's famous dictum that patriotism is the last resort of a scoundrel. In "Americanisms," he humorously maintained America's inalienable right to modify and develop the American language. Among his original narratives are "Walbridge," which is partly autobiographical, "The Lost Traveler," and "The Adventures of Henry Bird," the true story of a Virginian who settled in Ohio. Bird was captured by the Indians, was carried to Canada, and after several years was ransomed for a gallon of rum. He came to Washington to seek relief for sixty captured white women, and related his personal experiences to Paulding in the summer of 1815. Paulding indulged his fancy for fairies, ghosts, and mythology in "May-Day' and "Cupid and Hymen—An Allegory." In the latter, a beautiful thing, Jove sends Cupid and Hymen to bless mankind; but mankind banish Cupid, who ascends to Venus, while Hymen, the mortal, remains, his glory and loveliness departed.

Of Paulding's manner of life and associations early in 1815 one gets a pleasant glimpse from Hiram Paulding, a relative, then a boy of eighteen, who later became an admiral in the American navy.

"At the close of the war with England," [wrote Hiram in 1873] "I left Lake Champlain and found myself in New York without employment . . . and, in my earnest desire to join the fleet then nearly ready to sail, sought the friendly interest of James K. Paulding, who with Washington Irving, Commodore Decatur, Lieut. Jack Nicholson, Henry Brevoort, one of the literary clique, and some others lived with Mrs. Bradish, whose house fronted the Battery, forming a joyous fraternity." [9]

[9] *Life of Hiram Paulding* by Rebecca Paulding Meade (1910), p. 296.

By 1815 Paulding's writings, though anonymous and chiefly political, had attracted considerable attention. For three years, as we have seen, he had been a contributor to the *The Analectic Magazine* of Philadelphia, making a naval record of the War of 1812 and at times taking a fling at the British travelers and critics of America. His good-natured *John Bull and Brother Jonathan* had been republished and favorably reviewed in England; his narrative poem, *The Lay of the Scottish Fiddle,* had won the double distinction of a republication in London and a merciless scalping in *The Quarterly Review* for January, 1814. In the same number C. J. Ingersoll's *Inchiquin's Letters* (1810), a favorable account of the United States, occasioned another unmitigated censure of America, which with the savage review of his own poem heated Paulding's wrath to the boiling point. Immediately he began to assemble material for a systematic defence of the United States, and published it early in 1815 under the title *The United States and England.* Whatever effect this argumentative thunderbolt may have had on the relations between the two nations just then making peace, it had far-reaching influence on the author's future work. It was favorably reviewed and quoted by American publications, and it caught the admiring eye of President Madison, who at once set about finding a federal position worthy of the author's acceptance. Accordingly, in April, 1815, Paulding was appointed secretary of the newly created Board of Navy Commissioners at an annual salary not to exceed two thousand dollars, and began an eight-year residence in the pioneer city of Washington.

CHAPTER IV

DEFENDER OF THE UNITED STATES

WHEN the thirteen colonies won their independence and established the American Republic, the monarchies of the Old World, especially the mother country, England, watched the new venture with gloomy forebodings. England felt toward the new nation as a proud, domineering father feels toward a spirited child that flees from the paternal roof to enter into unapproved wedlock. With French aid, having won the war for independence, the United States wished to finish her new home and set things in order, but, while doing so, she was dragged into a long-standing war of words, of misrepresentation and gossip-mongering,—a sort of literary guerrilla contest, in which England was unquestionably the aggressor. The principal offenders were a number of English travelers, who visited the new land, crude and undeveloped, and returned to England with voluminous and usually projudiced accounts of what they had seen and heard. With few exceptions, they were chronic fault-finders. The more sensational they were, the better their books sold in England as well as in America. Their name was legion; in the preparation of the admirable and illuminating volume, *The English Traveller in America, 1785–1835*, Dr. Jane Louise Mesick examined seventy-five authors for the period of fifty years covered by her research. Though this Anglo-American controversy reached its climax in the administrations of Madison and Monroe, it really extended from the Revolution to the Great War, as the debate in the United States

46

Senate on the League of Nations proved. Such prominent authors as Thomas Moore, Robert Southey, Harriet Martineau, Frances M. Trollope, and Charles Dickens in England, and Timothy Dwight, James Fenimore Cooper, James K. Paulding, and Nathaniel P. Willis in America were drawn into some phase of the literary war. By virtue of an extraordinary tact and self-restraint, Washington Irving, except for a single diplomatic essay in *The Sketch-Book*, avoided the dispute, and by his winsome books and by his personal influence among such English writers as Scott and Gifford, surpassed all his contemporaries in promoting good will between the two nations. Near the end of the century, Irving's conciliatory method was followed in Bryce's *American Commonwealth*, which fostered Anglo-American friendship by fairly interpreting the people and institutions of the United States both to Englishmen and to Americans.

This battle of words was more than a figure of speech. So impregnated were the English with mistaken notions of the Americans that even Robert Southey in a letter to W. S. Landor in 1812 thus delivered himself: "They [the Americans] have in the course of twenty years acquired a distinct national character for low and lying knavery; and so well do they deserve it that no man ever had any dealings with them without having proofs of its truth." [1]   In 1851 an alert French scholar, Philarète Chasles, who had read some twenty of the controversial volumes, thus summarized his impressions:

"Every year, fresh British travellers cross the ocean, to see the progress of their grand-children. These latter, in their turn, pass the Atlantic, . . . look closely at their old mother, and hope to avenge themselves on her, and to find in her, faults, vices,

[1] Quoted by W. B. Cairns in *British Criticisms of American Writings, 1783–1815*, p. 11.

and absurdities.   Each does his work, the aristocrats try to
prove that the democracy is vicious and *vice-versa*: the young
vainly battles with the old; Marryat, Hall, Martineau, Trollope,
Dickens, have fired upon Americans; Cooper, Willis, and others
return it.   Irving, the man of taste, treats his English fathers
with filial kindness." [2]

Paulding is not listed here probably because he belonged
to the band of early defenders and withdrew from the
contest about 1825 after winning the main fight.

Most of the contestants could adequately vent their
spleen in a volume or two, but Paulding, partly from
personal inclination and partly perhaps from the conviction that he had been especially commissioned to guard
America, wrote five works in the famous controversy.   Indeed, so zealous was he for ten years in prosecuting the
literary war that his friends, Irving and Brevoort, concluded that he would be satisfied with nothing less than
the overthrow of the British Empire.   Fortunately, he
began and ended in a humorous vein.   His first treatment
of the theme was *The Diverting History of John Bull and
Brother Jonathan* (1812), which was so free from bitter
feeling and so diverting as to sell pretty well in both
nations.   (See Chapter III, pp. 39–42.)   The second was
The United States and England (1815), a vigorous
argumentative defence of the American nation.   His next
publication, *Letters from the South* (1817), belongs with
his other apologetic works, because it attempted to picture
one section of the country as it really was and because it
contained many references to the controversy.   After an
interval, Paulding returned to the subject in *A Sketch of
Old England* (1822).   In this he out-Englished the British
travelers by attempting to write a description of their

---

[2] Chasles' *Anglo-American Literature and Manners,* p. 148 (Scribner, New York, 1852).

country without even visiting it, but, in the midst of the book, he switched over to philosophical and literary criticism and gave his impressions of the principal English authors. In the last reply, *John Bull in America, or, The New Munchausen* (1825), he returned to his original humorous method, and was all the more effective because he used burlesque and satire. Thereafter his anti-British sentiments cropped out only casually. In his fiction, however, owing to his antipathy to Englishmen, his attempts to depict them usually ended in caricature.

In his *Letters from the South* (Vol. 2, p. 131) Paulding thus explains his attitude on the question to his imaginary correspondent:

"In the first place, you accuse me of hostility to English people, and English literature, because I speak, I hope, with becoming feelings, of the unceasing attempts of a great number of British writers, to injure the reputation of our countrymen and government in the eyes of the world. I disclaim the imputation of any other but defensive hostility; at the same time, I assure you, I am neither ashamed of feeling indignant at their calumnies, nor afraid of expressing my indignation. Whether abuse of the people of this country, its manners, morals, and literature is a popular subject or not; or whether it assures to the calumniator the patronage of government, I am not able to say; but certain it is, that there is hardly a newspaper or political pamphlet, published in that country, favourable to the ministerial side, that does not in some part of it contain a repetition of splenetic effusions against us. If the Reviewers get hold of an American publication, it is made use of merely as a pretext to calumniate us in some way or other; and one of the most celebrated of their Reviews seems to have been established for hardly any other purpose, than to libel America and France. It is called the Quarterly Review, and being rather an obscure, contemptible kind of a Billingsgate production, would hardly merit attention, were it not for its propensity to general and indiscriminate abuse of anybody the ministry dislikes."

The full title of the work that won Paulding his naval

position in Washington was *The United States and England: Being a Reply to the Criticism on Inchiquin's Letters, contained in the Quarterly Review for January, 1814*. Now, *Inchiquin, The Jesuit's Letters* (1810), written anonymously by Charles Jared Ingersoll, an American, was a calm, well-reasoned defence of the United States. The author defended the characters of Adams and Jefferson; he reviewed with discrimination two recent American publications, Barlow's *Columbiad* and Marshall's *Life of Washington;* he analyzed the commercial spirit of America.

"An affectation of contempt for America," wrote the fictitious Jesuit, "is one of the only prejudices in which all the nations of Europe seem to concur. The soil, climate, productions, and creatures of this enviable country have been stigmatized as altogether inferior to those of Europe. . . . The soil has been represented as parsimonious and abortive; the climate as froward and pernicious; the creatures as stunted, stupid, and debased below their species; the manners, principles, and government as suited to this universal depravity." [3]

Four years later *The Quarterly Review* made this innocent book the excuse for another unjustified denunciation of America, which at the time was generally, but erroneously, attributed to Robert Southey. Within a year it drew vindicating replies from Paulding and Timothy Dwight, president of Yale College. Paulding's volume took the field first, and was favorably reviewed by the *National Intelligencer* of Washington on January 17, 1815.

"The lover of his country, [runs the article] we think will find a rich treat in the perusal of this little work, which is written in the true attic spirit. It is a complete vindication of our country from the foul aspersions of the British hireling writers; and it not only vindicates, but it turns all their ribaldry, by proof positive derived from their own writers, upon their own country. At the same time that it is severe, it preserves that chaste, classic

[3] *Inchiquin, The Jesuit's Letters,* pp. 164–165.

DEFENDER OF THE UNITED STATES
James K. Paulding, aged about Thirty-five

From copy of an engraving made by F. Halpin from a drawing by Joseph Wood

and gentlemanly decorum that makes proof doubly felt, because it is uttered without passion and without abuse."

Paulding's work was also reviewed and copiously quoted in the initial number of *The North American Review* (May, 1815).

For his reply Paulding had made careful preparation. Internal evidence shows that he had spent nearly a year in gathering material and writing his defence, which would make an acceptable dissertation in political and social science. His analysis of the offensive review showed that the attack was directed at American politics, morals, manners, taste, literature, and religion, and to these criticisms he made a systematic reply. He wished to represent all sections of the United States, and vigorously objected to the discriminating patriotism shown by an eastern paper, which had published a series of articles admitting most of the charges provided New England were excepted. After reviewing the causes, progress, and outcome of the Revolution, Paulding described the English reviews, and expressed the opinion that the objectionable article was an attempt to get revenge for a recent congressional investigation into atrocities practiced by the British soldiers who had invaded this country. Of course, the burning of the Capitol was then a red-letter event. Next he demonstrated the unveracity of the three travelers quoted in *The Quarterly*, characterizing the third, Thomas Moore, as a perverted genius and the author of naughty songs. He showed that the principal, recurring fallacy in the article was the drawing of general conclusions from single incidents. To this sort of reasoning he replied in kind, citing an inkstand battle to discredit the British Parliament. To the accusation that American prisoners in American jails had been devoured by rats, Paulding retorted that it was doubtful whether a rat could exist in an English prison. His conjecture that the attack on America was intended to discourage emigration from England to this country was probably true. He concluded the volume with a brief defence of American literature.

In order to serve as secretary of the Board of Navy Commissioners, Paulding removed to the District of Columbia. In comparison with New York, the Washington of 1815 must have appeared to most people desolate and unattractive. In August of the preceding summer, the capitol, the president's house, and the war and treasury offices had been burned by the British. Though the city claimed a population of ten thousand, many of its inhabitants were itinerant legislators and diplomats; and according to Paulding, there were at least one thousand women "too lazy to work and too stupid to read," who converted the town into such a tattling place that a bachelor like himself could not put on a clean shirt, or pay a visit, or speak to a lady without convoking a tea-party to discuss the matter. The city had been planned but not built. It was nicknamed the "Wilderness City" and "City of Streets without Houses." When Congress was not in session, Irving found Washington a desert, melancholy place. But, though there were sometimes mud and weeds along Pennsylvania Avenue, Paulding discovered much to admire, for the city was beautifully situated, bird life was abundant, and deer were plentiful nearby. The thousand volumes in the Washington Library he could supplement by finding books in the primeval forests and ancient waterways. A poem named "Anadostan" is reminiscent of his life there:

> "There is a little grassy isle
> That parts Potomac's ample tide,
> Where Nature wears her gayest smile,
> And Nature's choicest sweets abide.
> 　　*　　　*　　　*　　　*

"The great trees, nodding to and fro
In stately conclaves not a few,
Whisper as secretly and slow
As bashful lovers ever do.

"The wild birds sing their roundelay,
For no rude sportsman spoils their glee,
And, all the live-long summer day,
Delight the ear with minstrelsy.

"And oh! how sweet the roses bloom,
And sweet the ruddy clover spreads,
And, springing from earth's fruitful womb,
How thick the violets lift their heads!" [4]

Paulding had not only a pleasant position but an opportunity to meet national leaders. To Irving he wrote of the former:

"It gives me leisure, respect, and independence, which last is peculiarly gratifying from its novelty. All my life I have been fettered by poverty, and my vivacity checked by the hopelessness of the future. Now, my spirits are good, my prospects fair, and the treatment I receive from all around is with [sic] respectful consideration. . . . The President is very friendly to me in deportment and little attentions, and so are the rest of the magnificos, particularly the Secretary of the Navy, who smokes my segars in the politest manner imaginable."

In letters to Henry Brevoort he expressed a longing for his old friends, and, referring to official subserviency in Washington, rated himself the only independent man there excepting the President.

Paulding became a close friend of Madison, and at the end of his presidency accompanied him to his Virginia home, where the next summer he spent several weeks, smoking, viewing the Blue Ridge, riding, chatting, joking,

---

[4] *Literary Life of J. K. Paulding,* pp. 186–188.

and exchanging stories. From the ex-president he learned
the private history of many important transactions.
Paulding considered him the sage of his time, with less
genius than Jefferson but with more nicely balanced
faculties. This friendship and a comparison of the literary
style of *The Federalist* with that of *The United States and
England* show that the two men had much in common.
Paulding also renewed his acquaintance with the famous
Virginia orator, John Randolph of Roanoke, whose novel
eloquence and striking personality had enchanted him.

In the summer of 1816 Paulding went by boat to Norfolk and thence by horseback on a leisurely journey for
his health to the Virginia springs, returning to Washington
late in the fall. The literary fruit of this excursion was
two rambling volumes entitled *Letters from the South*,
published in 1817. He first visited Yorktown and Richmond, paying a fine compliment to the lovely landscape
below Richmond, and praising the culture and liberality
of the Virginia planters as contrasted with a sordid, ma-
terialistic spirit he had observed elsewhere in the nation.
"The City of Richmond," he wrote, "deserves to have a
song written about it." On a previous journey he had
read with delight William Byrd's manuscript books. After
crossing the Blue Ridge into the Valley of Virginia, he
explored the wonders of Weir's Cave, observed the industrious life of the valley pioneers, many of them Ger-
mans, and passed on to the Warm and Hot Springs, then
frontier summer resorts chiefly for invalids. His journey
westward ended at the White Sulphur and Sweet Springs,
now in West Virginia, where he tarried a few weeks.

On his way from the sea to the mountains, Paulding observed people and customs sharply when he was not
closeted with his own meditations on Captain John Smith,
Yorktown, the British Reviews, American poetic literature,

and many similar topics. With interested but unprejudiced eyes, he saw both the bright and the black aspects of the institution of slavery. On a great plantation owned by a descendant of William Byrd, he found an illustration of the happier side of slave life—

"The plantation is large; containing, I believe, between nine and ten thousand acres; and several hundred negroes are attached to it. Some of the females are employed in taking care of the children, or in household occupations; others in the fields; while the old ones enjoy a sort of otium cum dignitate, at their quarters. These quarters consist of log cabins, disposed in two rows on either side a wide avenue, with each a little garden, in which they raise vegetables. White-washed and clean, they exhibited an appearance of comfort, which, in some measure served to reconcile me to bondage." [5]

In another passage he drew this picture of a slave trader and his possessions: [6]

"The sun was shining out very hot—and in turning an angle of the road, we encountered the following group: First, a little cart, drawn by one horse, in which five or six half naked black children were tumbled, like pigs, together. The cart had no covering—and they seemed to have been actually broiled to sleep. Behind the cart marched three black women with head, neck, and breasts uncovered, and without shoes or stockings; next came three men, bare-headed, half naked, and chained together with an ox-chain. Last of all came a white man—a white man! Frank—on horseback, carrying pistols in his belt, and who, as we passed him, had the impudence to look us in the face without blushing. I should like to have seen him hunted by bloodhounds. At a house where we stopped a little further on, we learned, that he had bought these miserable beings in Maryland, and was marching them in this manner to some one of the more southern States. Shame on the State of Maryland! I say—and shame on the State of Virginia!—and every State through which this wretched cavalcade was permitted to pass! Do they expect that

[5] Vol. 1, pp. 23–24.
[6] Vol. 1, pp. 128–129.

such exhibitions will not dishonour them in the eyes of strangers, however they may be reconciled to them by education and habit?"

In general, he observed that the country was thinly settled; and that the springs attracted only courageous invalids; yet along the difficult roads rolled covered wagons bearing ambitious settlers to the Ohio and Mississippi valleys; and in the mountain regions the pioneers, combining the arts of fishing, hunting, and farming, lived strenuous, independent, and happy lives. Facing the stern and bare realities of life in a wilderness, people had little leisure for architecture. Consequently, that Lexington, Virginia, boasted even a brick church and a brick courthouse called for special comment. In the South, as well as in almost every other section of the United States, Paulding noticed also an almost total absence of music. "In their love of music and poetry," he wrote (Volume II, page 221), "our countrymen are certainly behindhand with the people of Europe." The reason, he thought, was pioneer hard labor, which is the parent not only of "all the hardy virtues" but of "a sordid indifference to the finer impulses of the mind." His idea that physical labor impedes mental growth would hardly be acceptable to such philosophers as Carlyle, Emerson, and Thoreau.

In those early days palatial accommodations at the springs and modern railroad facilities were, of course, undreamed of. Paulding found at the White Sulphur Springs white-washed cabins built of square logs and arranged in rows on the edges of a little lawn. There one could develop a robust appetite for mutton and venison; and though there was plenty to eat, he complained that he could not properly masticate and swallow his food in the fifteen minutes allowed for meals—a statement of time not to be taken too seriously. His final observations on the mode of life at the springs are worth noting:

"As I am about leaving all the springs, hot and cold, bitter and sweet, I will say a few words to you about the modes of living at all that I have as yet visited. It is to be premised that very few people visit these springs, remote and difficult of access as they are, except to avoid the autumnal season, which is unhealthy in the low-lands; or in the hope of arresting the progress of some dangerous malady. Few come there for pleasure—and still fewer to exhibit their fine clothes. Indeed the greater proportion of the company consists of invalids; and, of course, little amusement or gayety is to be found at these places. Bathing, drinking the waters, eating, and sleeping, are the principal occupations; and for recreation, they sometimes dance of evenings—when there is any music.

"It is well they have this amusement, else they would be sadly put to it; for there is at none of these springs a drawing room, where such of the company as choose may meet for social purposes, either at morning or evening. The ladies live in cabins, most of them containing but one room—which, of course, has a bed in it—and we Americans are not yet in that pure state of Parisian innocence that we can visit a lady in her bedroom, without considerable—trepidation. Thus the only social place of meeting is at the spring; and there few opportunities for conversation occur. A neat, capacious, and well-furnished drawing-room would add infinitely to the pleasures of these fashionable resorts." [7]

On his return, Paulding recrossed the Alleghanies, veered south to Fincastle, and then north down the Valley of Virginia by the Natural Bridge, Lexington, Staunton, Winchester, and Berkeley Springs, which he pronounced as gay, as fashionable, and as often frequented as any watering place in America. When he drew near, late in the evening, he saw rambling among the trees at least a hundred gay people of both sexes, most of them from Maryland and Virginia. There was a drawing-room, which he had missed elsewhere, dancing, and pleasant walks about the spring. Over it was a pavilion, and there was

[7] Vol. I, pp. 231–233.

the luxury of two bath houses. In brief, "all the airs, graces, paraphernalia, caprices, and elegancies of the most fashionable assembly."[8]

Though less well known and less rich in detail than Timothy Dwight's contemporary *Travels in New England and New York*, or Jefferson's earlier *Notes on the State of Virginia*, yet Paulding's *Letters from the South* belong in the same class. Dwight is more concrete and voluminous; Jefferson, more exact and scholarly. In the main, Paulding's letters are discursive essays and descriptions of natural scenes, with little narration. Though based on limited observation and unduly drawn out into two volumes, these essay-letters, patriotically conceived and honestly written, will be increasingly valuable as a record of travel in the South in 1816, as an interpretation of national movements and dangers, and as a partial statement of Paulding's social and literary opinions.

In April, 1818, Paulding was living pleasantly with Commodore Porter, a member of the Board of Navy Commissioners, who had built a stately residence overlooking the Potomac; and there, in spite of ill health—lassitude and headaches—he indulged his taste for writing, which was rapidly becoming his vocation. For several months he had been sketching a narrative in heroic couplets, *The Backwoodsman*, which was published in the latter part of 1818. It is the story of an early settler on the Ohio, with descriptions of natural scenes and of Indian warfare. The author's ill health is reflected in the gloomy mood of the poem. It was severely, though unfairly, criticised by the Croaker wits, Joseph Rodman Drake in *The Evening Post* (New York, March 18, 1819) and Fitz-Greene Halleck in his poem entitled *Fanny* (1819). Halleck, however, commended the author's ability as a satirist. Their jovial crit-

[8] Vol. II, p. 237.

icism of Paulding resembles Byron's superficial criticism of Wordsworth. To say the least, the poem was creditable, and proved there was poetical stuff in the author. In a letter to Irving two years later he thus referred to it:

"My unfortunate poem has been over and over again attacked by the combined powers of wit and dullness. . . . Had I not been built of stubborn oak, seasoned in the school of poverty, like an old chimney piece in a log house, I should sometimes have scratched my head a little to find if I had any brains." [9]

Though the author attempted no long poem afterwards, he occasionally composed short pieces, which appeared either in his prose works or in the magazines.

On November 15, 1818, after a two-year engagement he married Gertrude Kemble, the sister of his friend, Gouverneur Kemble, and the daughter of a well-to-do merchant of New York. According to his son William he was as fortunate in the choice of his wife as he had been in the character of his mother. Since he was then forty years of age and well established in his bachelor habits of solitude and economy, he probably accustomed himself to an enlarged budget with some difficulty. It appears that Peter Kemble expressed his approval of the match by giving his daughter a small three-story brick house on Pennsylvania Avenue at a point then called "The Seven Buildings," where the Pauldings were residing in 1820.

In May, 1819, Irving and Paulding appeared before the American public as competitors. Each unaware of the other's plan launched a serial publication; Paulding alone began a Second Series of Salmagundi; Irving with trepidation published in the United States and England, where he was then living, the first edition of *The Sketch-Book*. Irving, putting forth his best effort and toiling in revision,

[9] *Literary Life,* p. 95.

won a chorus of praise on both sides of the Atlantic: Paulding, with a federal position to attend to, working hastily on such material as he could find, produced a lengthy volume, which in spite of many delightful pages was eclipsed by Irving's unique masterpiece.

Paulding had attempted so much, and in expressing his opinions showed himself so independent and fearless of public opinion, that the venture could not hope to be a popular success, though it contains some excellent humor and wise reflections. He had not yet learned the fine art of scrubbing public opinion without irritating the epidermis. The first seven numbers satirized fashionable society, luxury, false taste, English travelers, and dandies, but with less vivacity than in the first *Salmagundi;* in the last six numbers his satiric arrows sought fresh game in the new methods of education without study, in get-rich-quick lotteries, in street improvements that benefited rich officials at the expense of the poor, in paper money and easy bank loans, and in mistaken philanthropy. Scattered through the numbers are descriptions of nature and several character sketches; the fictitious letters show a lively interest in all kinds of people. In No. 6 there is a humorous account of the barnyard economy and cross-breeding experiments of a prosperous Dutchman, Henry Brevoort's father, who was a favorite with the author; other sections celebrate the wholesome pleasures of country life; Cockloft Hall is revisited, and the death of Old Caesar elicits a pathetic passage. In numbers 11 and 13 the imaginary visit of King Cornelius of the Oneida Indians to England and France occasions the best humorous narrative in the volume; here the author enjoyed himself to the peak in demonstrating comically the superiority of Indian society and government to those of Europe. This skit reminds one somewhat of Mark Twain's *Innocents Abroad.*

In the last number, in an important essay called "National Literature," Paulding anticipated Emerson by making his own declaration of literary independence, and championed realism by setting forth his theory of "rational fictions," which will be explained in Chapters V and VI.

The manner in which Paulding's work was being received by the critics, and Irving's opinion of it are reflected in the following letter of Irving to Henry Brevoort, from London, March 27, 1820:

"I had a delightful letter from James Paulding lately, dated from Washington; it brought so many recollections of early times and scenes and companions and pursuits to my memory, that my heart was filled to overflowing. What I would give to live over a few of the happy hours we have passed together! I am happy to find from Paulding's letter that he is pleasantly situated at Washington, and comfortable in his circumstances. There seems to be a pitiful and illiberal spirit indulged towards him by the writers in our reviews and newspapers. What is the state of our literature that it can afford to treat with slight and contumely such a writer as Paulding—there is no one that has ever portrayed American scenery and characters with greater truth and beauty. It is an ungenerous and unkind thing to put him and me in contrast, as some have done, and to praise me at his expense. It is excessively painful to me, and unjust to him. I neither deserve, nor desire distinction of that kind, and those that make it do not understand our distinct and comparative merit." [10]

For a year and a half after the publication of the last number of Salmagundi the Second on August 19, 1820, Paulding attempted no major literary work, but apparently he began a critical survey of the English government, society, and literature. In particular, he appears to have re-examined the principal English authors either for

[10] *Letters of Washington Irving to Henry Brevoort*, Vol. II, pp. 122–123.

self-cultivation or in preparation for his next book, and he looked critically into the social life of England as revealed in the writings of her own observers. Meantime, he published occasional sketches in *The National Intelligencer* of Washington over the pseudonym "Parvus Homo."

His next venture, *A Sketch of Old England by a New England Man* (New York and London, 1822), is a book of travels, fiction, and social and literary criticism. It consists of thirty-two letters, which purport to have been written from London to the author's brother in New York. The announced purpose was to draw a comparison between the English government, laws, and customs, and those of the United States. Through a dozen letters, the author tried to write as a traveler, either inventing the necessary details or omitting them, as, for example, in the case of Stratford-on-Avon, on the ground that Irving had recently described it. Thereafter, from London he wrote a medley on religion, theaters, politics, the nobility, poorhouses, pensions, books, authors, and so on. He touched nearly every phase of English life, usually indicating the superiority of America. Had Paulding's strictures been based upon actual knowledge of contemporary conditions in England, they might have anticipated Carlyle's *Past and Present,* which they often resemble.

The book provoked a criticism from *The Quarterly Review* for January, 1824, which correctly attributed the authorship to Paulding, and conjectured that he had not been in England and that the book was "a mere compilation from radical newspapers, treasonable pamphlets, blasphemous libels," and so on. In a letter to Evert A. Duyckinck in 1854, Paulding explained that his work was conceived in "a spirit of retaliation," and was full of gall and bitterness, and that he did not wish to see it revived. A Scotch reviewer, however, praising the author's vigor of intellect and skill in replying to his British critics, ventured a prediction that came true:

"The book is written with great talent. The author has the acuteness of Simond without his fastidiousness, with a greater grasp of intellect, and greater boldness and decision of character. His style is clear, nervous, abounding in figures and allusions full of vivacity, but easy, flowing, and unlabored. He cannot be long unknown, and when he comes forth will be entitled to take his place among the most powerful writers of the day in either continent. . . . He has avenged the injuries of England in a style which must turn the laugh against us in America, and would probe John Bull's self-love to the quick, if it could reach him." [11]

After publishing his first novel, *Koningsmarke*, in 1823, and removing to New York, Paulding directed his last major satiric attack against the English traveler in a burlesque volume called *John Bull in America; or, The New Munchausen* (New York and London, 1825). Though hastily written in three weeks, it contained sufficient wit and humor to attract favorable attention in the United States and in England. Like Knickerbocker's *A History of New York*, the preface pretended that the manuscript had been discovered in a room in a Washington hotel, mysteriously vacated by two travelers, an Englishman and a Frenchman. These characters flit about from place to place like the figures in the early movie plots; the action is highly fantastic, and to a modern reader the book seems to be wasted effort. Contemporaries, however, state that the satire was effective. The keynote of the volume was

[11] Quoted in a volume entitled "A letter to the editor of The Edinburgh Political and Literary Journal; in reply to the Article in that Newspaper of 22d January, 1823, . . . By Philopolis." London, Printed for T. and G. Underwood, 32, Fleet Street, 1825. (Taken from a copy of the book in the Harvard Library, pages 13–14 and 33–34).

sounded by such repeated phrases as "turbulent spirit of democracy," "total disregard of religion," and the "spitting, gouging, drinking, duelling, dirking, swearing, strutting republicans." According to the satire, the habit of smoking tobacco was so prevalent among men, women, and children in America, that, when autumn came, the people would begin a smoking festival that lasted five or six weeks, and the atmosphere would become so smoky and dark that they must burn candles all day; and this season was called Indian Summer! A briefer, saner, and equally humorous characterization of the United States Paulding published in the *New York Mirror* for September 10, 1825, under the title "Brother Jonathan." In his writings thereafter, references to the literary war were incidental.

These five major replies to the British critics of the United States were effective and brought Paulding public favor and reputation. "No individual," wrote the editor of the *New York Mirror* for May 5, 1832, "has more contributed to bring them [English travelers] to their proper level, and to connect them in a thousand ways with burlesque and ludicrous associations, than Mr. Paulding." By 1825 he observed that England was showing a more kindly feeling toward the United States, and, though he was still a loyal defender, he was willing to admit that Brother Jonathan was by no means perfect. After commending his enterprise, inventiveness, and good humor, Paulding continued in this vein:

"Jonathan is no great patron of literature. He encourages the publication of newspapers, editions of the Bible, and the 'dying confessions' of malefactors; but for the higher walks of genius, he has, in general, no relish. And yet, unaccountable as it may seem, he has a greedy appetite for John's novels and reviews—especially for the latter when well seasoned with abuse of himself." [12]

[12] *New York Mirror*, September 10, 1825.

Some years later, when Harriet Martineau visited America, Paulding acted as if he wished to avoid further involvement in the controversy. Though she was eager to interview him, called many times to see him, and even trailed him to Kemble's home near West Point, yet he steadfastly refused to meet her, and in a conversation with a friend he drew a graphic picture of the deaf English lady with her long ear-trumpet, collecting the materials for her *Society in America* (1837).[13]

Paulding's controversial period, extending from 1815 to 1825, almost coincides with his first residence in Washington. Soon after the death of his father-in-law in July, 1823, he resigned the secretaryship of the Navy Board and returned to New York. Mrs. Paulding had inherited the Kemble house in Whitehall Street and several tracts of land in New York and New Jersey. Though the family had planned to settle in New Jersey, Paulding resumed residence in New York, for in January, 1824, he was appointed navy agent for New York by President Monroe. The position was all the more agreeable, because it was an unsolicited gift from the President, who had been besieged by fifty-three candidates. Retaining Mr. George L. Storer, ex-navy agent, as his chief clerk, who attended to the details of the office, Paulding had much leisure for writing, and he entered upon a fruitful period of fourteen years, in which he produced chiefly fiction.

[13] L. G. Clark in *The Knickerbocker* for July, 1860; Vol. 56, p. 87.

CHAPTER V

AUTHOR OF SEVENTY TALES

WHEN Hawthorne and Poe, who are usually credited with perfecting the American short story, began to write in the early thirties, Paulding had already won distinction in this genre. During several years of experimentation he had produced a steady stream of stories, at least six of which had been republished in England. This chapter may succeed in showing that he contributed some valuable ideas to the short story.

In the period from 1823 to 1838 he came before the public chiefly as the author of tales and novels, which in contrast to the then fashionable romantic narratives he called "rational fictions." Not to mention a few simple stories published before 1820, his first major effort was a two-volume novel, *Koningsmarke* (1823), a story of the Delaware Swedes, written in imitation of *Tom Jones*. (See Chapter VI, pp. 95-97.) Then, after publishing the hasty satire, *John Bull in America* (1825), he began to experiment with the tale, as the form best fitted to the tastes of American readers and the needs of publishers. In the next decade, he averaged five or six stories annually, and published them either in the leading periodicals or in book form. Irving put forth no tales between 1824 and 1832; Hawthorne and Poe were yet apprentices; and the interval may be fairly named the Paulding decade of the short story.

Paulding's theory of "rational fictions" was set forth in the final number of *Salmagundi, Second Series,* August

19, 1820. In a critical essay entitled "National Literature," he rejected the prevalent notion that the United
States had scanty materials for fiction, and then explained
his conception of the perfect work of the imagination, the
"rational fiction":

"Wherever there are men, [he reasoned] there will be materials for romantic adventure. In the misfortunes that befall
them; in the sufferings and vicissitudes which are everywhere
the lot of human beings; in the struggles to counteract fortune,
and in the conflicts of the passions, in every situation of life,
he who studies nature and draws his pictures from her rich and
inexhaustible sources of variety, will always find enough of those
characters and incidents which give a relish to works of fancy.
The aid of superstition, the agency of ghosts, fairies, goblins, and
all that antiquated machinery which till lately was confined to
the nursery, is not necessary to excite our wonder or interest our
feelings. . . .

"The best and most perfect works of imagination appear to me
to be those which are founded upon a combination of such
characters as every generation of men exhibits, and such events
as have often taken place in the world, and will again. Such
works are only fictions, because the tissue of events which they
record never perhaps happened in precisely the same train, and
to the same number of persons, as are exhibited and associated
in the relation. Real life is fraught with adventures, to which
the wildest fictions scarcely afford a parallel; and it has this
special advantage over its rival, that these events, however
extraordinary, can always be traced to motives, actions, and
passions, arising out of circumstances no way unnatural, and
partaking of no impossible or supernatural agency."

He went on to point out that stories of this class, if
they are skillfully conducted, gratify both the judgment
and the fancy of the reader, whereas stories of supernatural beings in whom nobody believes satisfy only the imagination. He maintained, also, "that these probable and
consistent fictions" are much more difficult to manage than
"this machinery of ghosts, goblins, and fairies," who are

always present to aid the author and who are subject to no
rational motive or law of cause and effect. Praising the
practice of Henry Fielding and Charles Brockden Brown,
Paulding indicated the rich materials that the writer of
fiction could find in the American pioneers—in their character, motives, courage, perseverance, adventures, and contests with the Indians. The fact that this matter had
been so little used in early American fiction, he attributed
to a mistaken criticism, bad models, and a slavish imitation
of foreign literary styles. He advised the young candidate
for honors in fiction to eschew servile imitation, to think
and feel for himself, to follow nature, and to picture the
scenes and narrate the events connected with our pride and
affections. In this way, Paulding thought, an original
national literature could be established. With equal emphasis elsewhere in his writings he opposed the irrational
extravagance in the current romantic fiction, and championed the principles of realism.

Before Cooper had written any of his American novels,
Paulding's essay thus charted the field of American fiction,
and suggested principles upon which it could be successfully developed. Cooper, a man of action and a born story-
teller, in *The Spy* and *The Pioneers* was the first, perhaps
unwittingly, to exemplify these principles; Paulding's attempt in *Koningsmarke* came three years after his own
theory. Though in composing his essay he was quite evidently thinking of long narratives, and though his own
first trial thereafter was a novel in two volumes, still in
his tales he usually applied the same narrative principles.
Years later, however, he conveniently forgot his fictional
theory long enough to write an occasional ghost story and
a collection of fairy tales.

Many factors co-operated in the development of his fictional theories. First, he held an influential position that

yielded both adequate income and leisure for study and composition. After an absence of eight years in Washington,
he returned to his friends in New York City, where in
June, 1824, he was one of the sixty prominent persons to
organize the New York Athenaeum. Though he had
purged his thought of the Anglo-American dispute, he was
yet able to build on his reputation as a political writer.
In recognition of his literary work, Columbia College
in August, 1824, conferred upon him, as well as upon
Cooper and Webster, the degree of Master of Arts. Fortunately, in George P. Morris, editor of the weekly *New
York Mirror,* he found a true friend and helpful critic,
who reviewed his books judiciously and who on occasion
could advise Cooper to rewrite a novel. Besides, in the
flock of annuals and magazines then taking wing, there
was a demand for short sketches and native tales. Finally,
as the last of the Dutch houses in the city began to disap-
pear, he shared the popular interest in the city's past, and
by his writings won the title of New York's most eminent
Dutch antiquarian.

Paulding was also mature when he turned definitely to
fiction. He knew people; he could see beneath the surface
of things. In a very real sense, he had been educated by
nature, by books, and by association with men; and he was
still young enough to learn. Among authors, his favorites
were Shakespeare, Milton, Goldsmith, Dryden, Burns, and
Fielding. Byron and Moore he abhorred, but Scott and
Cooper he liked with reservations, and he esteemed Franklin and C. B. Brown. He was also well read in the current
English and American magazines. Then, as an independent thinker, he had confidence in himself and his opinions.
His rugged strength is reflected in the following consolation written to Irving in 1825:

"It gives me some little dissatisfaction to perceive that you suffer yourself to be influenced in the pursuit of a great object by the squibs and crackers of criticism. For my part, I have not, like you, been sufficiently praised to feel much the want of it; I am a hardened sinner; and if I know myself, care very little about the decisions of tribunals whose judgments can eventually have little influence on the opinions of posterity." [1]

Into his home life, also, had come the innocence of children and a great sorrow over their loss. Though four of his sons grew to manhood and survived him, he lost his oldest boy in 1825 after a long illness from some inscrutable disorder, and two years later he lost a second child. In December, 1827, Brevoort thus wrote Irving, "He [Paulding] and Gertrude have been in deep distress by this sudden event. He continues to live along in a quiet way, mixing seldom with society and occasionally producing a work of merit." [2]

In April of the same year, Irving thus wrote from Madrid to Henry Brevoort:

"I have not heard for some time past from Paulding. His last letters were full of kind feeling and interesting anecdotes. I am too glad to find that he is settled in the old homestead of the Kemble family, that scene of so many happy hours. As to his retired mode of life, I fancy it is the happiest when a man has a family for his world, books at his elbow and his pen as an amusement. I have not seen two or three of his late publications. All of those that I have met with bear his usual stamp of originality, his vein of curious and beautiful thought, his turns of picturesque language, mingled with the faults that arise from hasty and negligent composition. Early habit and associations have given a charm to his writings in my eyes; I always find in them passages that strike on some chord of old remembrance." [3]

1 *Life and Letters of Washington Irving* by P. M. Irving, Vol. 2, p. 239.

2 *Literary Life*, p. 184; *Letters of Henry Brevoort to Washington Irving*, Vol. 2, p. 14.

3 P. M. Irving's *Life and Letters of Washington Irving*, Vol. 2, p. 261.

For many years Paulding had been an attentive student of literary style. In a fine passage in *Letters from the South* he had denounced the unnatural, inflated English then in fashion. His own prose was later to win high praise. George P. Morris observed that it was adjusted to the subject and the occasion. In 1831, an English journal reviewing *The Dutchman's Fireside* thus commended him: "Mr. Paulding is neither too elaborate like Irving, nor diffuse like Cooper, nor wild, and almost frantic, like Neal; he is just, neat, fanciful, and descriptive." [4] And judging his style by his prose of this decade, Edgar Allan Poe wrote: "There is no better literary manner than the manner of Mr. Paulding. Certainly no American, and possibly no living writer of England, has more of those numerous peculiarities, which go to the formation of a happy style." [5]

Hitherto, the number and merit of his tales have been overlooked. Perhaps no other American author has been so abominably edited as Paulding, and owing to the mass of his experimental, political, and journalistic work, no one has so much needed an editor. Even his son's collection made in the sixties contained only one novel and four stories of any consequence hidden in a mass of journalistic matter; and the Harper edition of the thirties was even more censurable. Of course, the truth is that, had Paulding written half as much and twice as well as he wrote, he would be a leading American author; but he is entitled to be judged by his best work. It is, indeed, not surprising that his realistic, rational fictions should have been submerged by the tearful sentimentality so abundant in the decades before the Civil War. Even Hawthorne, Poe, Whitman, and Thoreau were for a time strangled

[4] *The Westminster Review*, Oct., 1831, Vol. 15, p. 491.
[5] Poe's Review of Paulding's *A Life of Washington* (1835).

by it, and emerged slowly and doubtfully. In 1855, when
Stowe's *Uncle Tom's Cabin*, Susan Warner's *Queechy*, and
Mitchell's *Reveries of a Bachelor* were selling by the hundred thousand, Hawthorne thus described the sentimental
invasion: "America is now wholly given over to a d——d
mob of scribbling women. I should have no chance of success while the public taste is occupied with their trash—
and should be ashamed of myself if I did succeed." [6]

Between 1807 and 1848, Paulding composed seventy-odd
short narratives. Of these, forty-eight appeared in the
decade 1826–1836, and most of the others after 1843. In
the interval he was Secretary of the Navy. When, therefore, Hawthorne and Poe began their work in the early
thirties, Paulding was probably the most prolific of American story tellers. In the same decade, Miss Catharine M.
Sedgwick's tales, though few, were popular. In the same
half century, according to Professor Pattee, Irving wrote
48 tales, Willis about 60, Hawthorne 110, and Poe 70. In
fertility, then, Paulding compares favorably with his contemporaries. At the end of this chapter is a list of his
tales chronologically arranged.

Perhaps the most important is the group of thirteen published in *The Atlantic Souvenir*, the first and leading annual in the United States; to each number for seven years,
beginning in 1826, Paulding contributed from one to three
tales. Seven of the lot are among his best, for he had
time to plan and compose them with care. Seven tales, including "The Yankee Roué," "The Dumb Girl," and
"The Politician," first appeared in book form. The larg-
est group, thirty, was published between 1830 and 1835
in the *New York Mirror*, perhaps the most influential
weekly publication of the period. Fifteen came out in

---

[6] Quoted by F. L. Pattee in *The Development of the American
Short Story*, pp. 149–150.

Graham's Magazine of Philadelphia in the forties. The others were scattered in books and magazines, and some are probably unidentified.

In two British collections of American tales edited by Mary Russell Mitford in 1830 and 1832, Paulding led with six stories in a total of thirty-five. In selecting them the editor showed sound judgment. The next in order were: five by James Hall, four by Miss Sedgwick, three each by G. C. Verplanck and William Leggett, two each by Willis and Bryant, and none by Irving, whose writings she held to be essentially European. Miss Mitford stated that the tales had been selected "principally from a great mass of Annuals, Magazines, and other periodicals, embracing many of the most popular productions of the most popular living writers of the Western World." [7] Paulding's leadership was also recognized at home by the compiler of *The Atlantic Club-Book* (1834), which contained selections from native authors. The volume was dedicated to James K. Paulding as the chief defender, promoter, and adorner of American letters.

On January 2, 1833, in consequence of a rumor that Paulding was to be displaced as navy agent at New York, his friend Washington Irving addressed a letter to Martin Van Buren at Albany, paying tribute to Paulding's character and services. In part Irving wrote:

"Paulding is a public man, known throughout the nation by his writings, which have ever inculcated the most patriotic and republican sentiments. He is a staunch and sincere friend to the administration and to the old general [President Jackson]. He is a most honorable high-minded man whose character gives a dignity to office. He is widely connected by marriage, and his connexions are all strong friends to the administration. He is moreover prized and blessed by a wide circle of friends of a

[7] Same, p. 45. See pp. 49–50 for contents of the British Collections.

class, standing and character to have an influence on society by their opinions. Such a man is valuable to a party by the very respectability of his character and conduct, but I know Paulding to be a very useful man by his pen, which he exerts anonymously, and merely for his own gratification, in the newspapers, on the administration side." [8]

The next day Irving visited President Jackson at Washington in reference to the report, and immediately he wrote to Paulding:

"I have just returned from an interview with the President on the subject of the rumor of your removal from office. He assured me it was the first word he had heard on the subject; and had you heard the terms in which he spoke of your official conduct, you would feel not merely secure of your office, but proud of holding it, guaranteed by such sentiments. The more I see of this old cock of the woods, the more I relish his game qualities." [9] . . .

Three years later Paulding had an opportunity to aid Edgar Allan Poe in his search for a publisher and at the same time to express his opinion of Poe's early work. In explanation two of Paulding's letters are here inserted. The first was addressed to T. W. White, editor of the *Southern Literary Messenger;* and the second, to Edgar A. Poe at Richmond.

(Letter to T. W. White)

"New York, March 3, 1836.

"Dear Sir—I duly received the book containing the tales by Mr. Poe heretofore published in the 'Messenger,' and have delayed writing to you on the subject until I could communicate the final decision of the Messrs. Harpers as to their republication. By the way, you are entirely mistaken in your idea of my influence over these gentlemen in the transactions of their

[8] Martin Van Buren's Correspondence in the Library of Congress.
[9] P. M. Irving's *Life and Letters of Washington Irving*, Vol. 3, pp. 46–47.

business. They have a Reader, by whose judgment they are guided in their publications, and like all other traders are governed by their anticipations of profit or loss, rather than any intrinsic merit of a work or its author. I have no influence in this respect, and indeed ought to have none, for my taste does not exactly conform to that of the public at present. I placed the work in their hands, giving my opinion of it, which was such as I believe I have heretofore expressed to you more than once, leaving them to their own decision.

"The [y] have finally declined republishing it for the following reasons: They say that the stories have so recently appeared before the public in the 'Messenger' that they would be no novelty—but most especially they object that there is a degree of obscurity in their application, which will prevent ordinary readers from comprehending their drift, and consequently from enjoying the fine satire they convey. It requires a degree of familiarity with various kinds of knowledge which they do not possess, to enable them to relish the joke: the dish is too refined for them to banquet on. They desire me, however, to state to Mr. Poe that if he will lower himself a little to the ordinary comprehension of the generality of readers, and prepare a series of original tales, or a single work, and send them to the publishers, previous to their appearance in the 'Messenger,' they will make such arrangements with him as will be liberal and satisfactory.

"I regret this decision of the Harpers, though I have not opposed it, because I do not wish to lead them into any measure that might be accompanied by a loss, and felt as I would feel for myself in a similar case. I would not press a work of my own on them, nor do I think Mr. Poe would be gratified at my doing so with one of his.

"I hope Mr. Poe will pardon me if the interest I feel in his success should prompt me to take this occasion to suggest to him to apply his fine humor, and his extensive acquirements, to more familiar subjects of satire; to the faults and foibles of our own people, their peculiarities of habits and manners, and above all to the ridiculous affectations and extravagancies of the fashionable English Literature of the day, which we copy with such admirable success and servility. His quiz on Willis, and the burlesque of 'Blackwood,' were not only capital, but what is more, were understood by all. For satire to be relished, it is necessary that it should be leveled at something with which readers are familiar. My own experience has taught me this, in the failure of some efforts of my own formerly.

"Be good enough to let me know what disposition I shall make of the work.

"I am respectfully,

"Your friend and servant,
"J. K. PAULDING." [10]

(Letter to Edgar A. Poe)

"New York, 17th March, 1836.

"Dear Sir—In compliance with your wishes, it would have afforded me much pleasure to propose the publication of your book to some one respectable bookseller of this city. But the truth is, there is only one other, who publishes anything but school books, religious works and the like, and with him, I am not on terms that would make it agreeable to me, to make any proposition of this nature, either in my own behalf or that of another. I have therefore placed your work in the hands of Messrs. Harpers to forward with a box of books they are sending to Richmond in a few days, and I hope it will come safely to hand.

"I think it would be worth your while, if other engagements permit, to undertake a tale in a couple of volumes, for that is the magical number. There is a great dearth of good writers at present both in England and this country, while the number of readers and purchasers of books, is daily increasing, so that the demand is greater than the supply, in mercantile phrase. Not one work in ten now published in England, will bear republication here. You would be surprised at their excessive mediocrity. I am of opinion that a work of yours would at least bring you a handsome remuneration, though it might not repay your labors, or meet its merits. Should you write such a work, your best way will be to forward the MS directly to the Harpers, who will be I presume governed by the judgment of their *Reader,* also from [sic] long experience can tell almost to a certainty what will succeed. I am destitute of this valuable

[10] *Life and Letters of Edgar Allan Poe,* by James A. Harrison, Vol. II, pp. 377-8 (Crowell, 1902-3).

instinct, and my opinion counts for nothing with publishers. In other respects you may command my good offices.

"I am Dr Sir,

"Your friend and serv^t,

"J. K. PAULDING." [11]

These letters show that Paulding recognized in young Poe a fellow satirist of the "ridiculous affectations and extravagancies of the fashionable English Literature of the day." To be more effective, he advised Poe to level his satire at subjects familiar to his readers. Paulding recognized Poe's "fine humor, and his extensive acquirements" as shown in ten or fifteen of his early stories. Observing "a great dearth of good writers at present both in England and this country," he also advised Poe to compose a two-volume tale. Then, he added judiciously, "I am of opinion that a work of yours would at least bring you a handsome remuneration, though it might not repay your labors, or meet its merits." Apparently, because of this advice to write a long story and because of the popular interest in the South Sea exploring expedition then being planned by the government, Poe began the composition of *The Narrative of Arthur Gordon Pym,* and published the first part of it in the *Southern Literary Messenger* for January and February, 1837.

THE TALES CLASSIFIED

With respect to the source of their material, Paulding's tales fall into two classes: eighteen foreign and fifty-odd American. Excepting two or three, the foreign stories are unreal and inconsequential. They are, probably, a concession to the popular interest in foreign themes aroused by

[11] Same, Vol. II, pp. 31–32.

Irving and Willis. The larger group treat native situa-
tions, ideas, and characters, and with these he did his best
work. Let us consider them in eight overlapping groups.

1. The most important are about fifteen tales which present Dutch characters, customs, and superstitions. Their
genuineness is impressive. To the same class belong his
best novels, *The Dutchman's Fireside* and *The Old Continental.* They represent work that only Paulding could
do and that no one can duplicate. In them he as certainly
interpreted the New York Dutch as Hawthorne in his fictions interpreted the Puritans. Paulding knew the Dutch
thoroughly, and though a Mohammedan or a Frenchman
might evade him, a Dutchman could not. Among the best
Dutch tales are: "Cobus Yerks," "The Dumb Girl," "The
White Indian," "Claas Schlaschenschlinger," "Yankee
Pedagogues and Dutch Damsels," "Knickerbocker Hall,"
and "The Revenge of St. Nicholas." Some are comic;
some are tragic; all are realistic. Though his art may be
imperfect, for Paulding was working in a new form with
no Fielding or Shakespeare to lead the way, yet the truth
of the portrayal can not be questioned. His Dutch psychology is sound.

Perhaps the best is "Cobus Yerks" (1828), in which the
scene is Tarrytown and the time, November, 1793. Little
Cobus, a Dutch farmer, drove a two-horse wagon to town
with produce and spent the day there. At the tavern, like
Tam o'Shanter, he drank and listened to ghost stories, especially one told by a witty Englishman who knew Cobus'
weakness for spooks, goblins, and fiends of all sorts, and
who in a sepulchral voice related that there was at large
a fiendish creature that howled like the devil incarnate.
Between these yarns and his liquor poor Cobus was scared
nearly out of his wits, and he hugged the tavern fireside
till all had left except the landlady, who finally ordered

him out and helped him to get started. The next day, when he did not return home, his neighbors began a search, and found his team, his wrecked wagon, and himself, bloody and apparently dead. When revived, he gave his version of what had happened, which is the best part of the story, reminding his hearers that he had been as sober as a deacon. This story is brief, concrete, plausible, picturesque, humorous, and true to the Dutch life of that time. Cobus and the Englishman are well drawn, and the tavern, kept by "a bitter root of a woman," is realistic.

2. About fifteen tales are humorous, satiric, or witty. Like Chaucer and Fielding, the author liked to present life humorously and to eradicate political, social, and literary follies by causing people to laugh at them. So he made the English traveler, the selfish politician, the society dandy, and the silly woman appear ridiculous. In "The Poet's Tale," which is a satire on the rage for Moore's and Byron's poetry, he wrote, "I always considered the eccentricities of mankind, as among the most amusing portions of the drama of human life." Accordingly, in "The Azure Hose," a novelette, he satirized false social and literary styles as exhibited by Lord Byron; in "Dyspepsy" he satirized the abuse of wealth and gluttony; and in "The Yankee Roué" he exposed traveled dandies. But these are not his best witty stories, for in them his ideas are imperfectly clothed in character and action. "Too Fast and Too Slow," a rollicking satire on youthful indecision and fickleness, and "The School of Reform," depicting a shrewish wife, are better. "Jonathan's Visit to the Celestial Empire" and "The Great Medicine, or The Magic Whiskers" are amusing farces. In these, of course, plot and characterization are negligible. They entertained his first readers, and they are still diverting. Those who question the author's wit should read these and also his humorous

papers, "Retiring from the Cares of Life," published in
Godey's Magazine. (Cf. Paulding's Criticism, Chap. 8.)

In this connection, it is worth noting that Poe's early
tales were satirical. According to his own statement,
"Lionizing" satirized the rage for "lions," and "Loss of
Breath" satirized the extravagances of *Blackwood's.*
Paulding thought that Poe's quiz on Willis and "Loss of
Breath" were capital, and recommended that his shafts be
aimed at subjects familiar to readers. "It would seem,
therefore," concludes Prof. Pattee, summarizing the evidence, "that Poe by his own confession and in the judgment of those of his contemporaries [Kennedy and Paul-
ding] best fitted to speak upon the matter considered these
early tales, including even 'Berenice' and 'Morella,' as
satires upon the philosophical vagaries of the time and
upon the extravagances of current prose romance." [12]

3. Many of the tales stress character. Several were
named for the principal actors. Consider: "The White
Indian," "Cobus Yerks," "Un Fainéant," "The Yankee
Roué," "The Drunkard," "The Millionaire," and "Poor
Genevieve." Even in these Paulding often used the comic
method. At the end of "The Politician" he explained,
"I have preferred to make my drama a farce rather than a
tragedy. I pretend not to any other authority than that
of experience; but I have seen enough of the world, and of
the people of the world, to know by experience, that beautiful as wisdom is, if she would only sometimes condescend
to smile, she would be irresistible." In depicting character he wasted no time on appearances; in *Westward Ho!*
he stated his opposition to overminute description as a
means of revealing character. He emphasized the motives
and the actions; accordingly, the reader often feels the

[12] F. L. Pattee's *The Development of the American Short Story*
(New York, 1923), p. 122.

presence of his characters rather than sees them. Note
the skill and verbal melody with which exposition, dialogue, and action are blended in the following passage
from "The Politician":

"One day I met Deliverance Brookfield, by chance, in a spot
where we had often played together in childhood, and walked
together in youth. She turned her head the other way, and was
passing me without notice. The sense of offending guilt over-
came for a moment the sublime theory of the Honorable Peleg,
and I involuntarily exclaimed, 'Miss Brookfield!'

"She turned upon me a countenance at once pale and beautiful, but tinged deeply with melancholy reproach, as she looked
steadily in my face without speaking.

" 'Have you forgot me, Miss Brookfield?'

" 'I believe I have,' at length she replied in a sad kind of
languor. 'I would never wish to remember one who has repaid
the friendship of my father, and the kindness of my mother, by
destroying our happiness.'

"I felt like a scoundrel, but mustered hypocrisy enough to
answer in a gay tone,

" 'My dear Miss Brookfield, nobody thinks any thing of such
trifles in politics; nothing but political squibs—forgot in a day
—They do no harm to anyone.'

" 'None?' she replied bitterly; 'no harm except murdering rep-
utations and breaking hearts. My father is dying.' And she
burst into tears.

" 'Dying!' cried I, 'Heaven forbid! of what?'

" 'Of the wounds you have given him. O George, George!'
continued she, 'you should come to our house, and receive a
lesson of what a few slanders can do in destroying the happiness
of an innocent family.'

"She passed on, and I had not courage to stop, or to follow
her. I went to the Honorable Peleg and gave him notice, that
it was my intention to retract all I had said or insinuated against
Mr. Brookfield, in the next day's Banner of Truth.

" 'And lose my election—I mean sacrifice a great principle, and
jeopardize the happiness of millions to a little private feeling
of compunction?' "

4. Many of the tales are didactic, and the author is no

mean teacher. Following the fashion and his own inclination, he often incorporated his ideas in stories. Like Ibsen,
Paulding frequently began a narrative with a proposition
to be clothed in characters and action. "Ghosts" and
"The Yankee Roué," "Brand" and "The Mother's Tragedy" have something in common. Paulding was first a
thinker and a critic and afterwards a story teller. In
"The Poet's Tale" he remarked, "A story with a moral
is always worth telling." In "The Victim of Trifles"
he inculcated the virtues of patience and industry; in
"The Two Clocks" he suggested mutual forbearance in
the marriage relation; in "The Mother's Tragedy," a
convincing story, he loosed a powerful bolt at fanaticism;
in "The Magic Spinning Wheel" he genially preached the
gospel of work, anticipating both Carlyle and Ruskin. In
this group belong also his apologues, such as "Cupid and
Hymen" and "Time and Truth."

5. Several tales are psychological. Paulding's love of
solitude reminds one of Hawthorne. In 1827, Brevoort
wrote Irving that his friend was living "a life of complete
seclusion." Thus he could observe the processes of his
own mind and reflect on the human drama around him.
His tale, "The Drunkard," reveals the slow degeneration
of a character. "The Mother's Tragedy" presents a form
of religious mania. "The Mother's Choice" and "The
Dumb Girl" center one's interest on the passion of love;
in the first, the mother chooses unwisely for her daughter;
in the second, the girl chooses unwisely for herself.

Special interest attaches to "The Dumb Girl" (1830),
because it resembles and may have influenced *The Scarlet
Letter* (1850). Hawthorne's omnivorous reading would
hardly miss a book of stories by an author so prominent
as Paulding. Again, in the introduction and conclusion of
his famous novel, Hawthorne emphasized his indebtedness

to Mr. Surveyor Pue, his "official ancestor." Now the
account of Mr. Pue, usually held to be pure fiction, fits
Paulding nicely. In very truth, in his day "a man's office
was a life-lease," for Paulding served the government for
forty years. Hawthorne's claim for "the authenticity of
the outline" and "the authority which we have chiefly
followed" fits these facts: that Paulding professed to be
only the editor, and not the author, of *Chronicles of the
City of Gotham,* in which "The Dumb Girl" was first published; and that Paulding really knew the girl at Tarrytown in his boyhood. Consider, too, that Hawthorne stated
that the girl's story was the theme of "long meditation"
and "much thought," and that in his *American Note-
Books* for September 7, 1835, the plot of "The Dumb Girl"
was thus accurately recorded:

"A young man to win the love of a girl, without any serious
intentions, and to find that in that love, which might have
been the greatest blessing of his life, he had conjured up a spirit
of mischief, which pursued him throughout his whole career—
and this without any revengeful purposes on the part of the
deserted girl."

Paulding's story in forty pages gives the main action,
and introduces the heroine, the seducer, a child, and con-
science or remorse, which Hawthorne personified in Chil-
lingworth. In both versions, the main action covers seven
years; in both, there are woodland scenes; in both, the
gossips act as a chorus; in both, the heroine is queenly, elegant in dress, self-reliant, industrious, and unselfish; in
both, the seducer deserts the heroine and is slowly stung
by remorse; in both, there are reconciliation and reunion
at the end. Psychologically, Paulding's tale is probably
stronger than Hawthorne's in that in "The Dumb Girl"
remorse for seduction is combined with remorse for being
implicated in the girl's apparent death. The fact, too,

that Hawthorne's other romances had considerable basis
in reality tends to support this claim for Paulding's influence. If this conjecture is correct, Hawthorne omitted the
idiot brother of the girl and the drowning episode; he
changed the setting from Tarrytown to Boston; he substi-
tuted the minister for the prodigal, a girl-child for a
boy; introduced symbolism, the scaffold, and the jail; and
elaborated the details in his own picturesque manner and
in harmony with the Puritan environment In "The Dumb
Girl," public opinion is faced by the seducer; in *The Scarlet Letter,* by the seduced. Paulding's tale, unhurried and
natural, exhibits a fine understanding of human nature,
and moves in the twilight zone of the spirit.

6. In some of his tales, plot is the main interest. Though
many were hastily written and are weak in plot, yet Paulding could weave a good story. Professor Pattee observed
that though they might be rambling, they contained "often really brilliant narrative and description." In "The
White Indian," "The Dumb Girl," "Cobus Yerks," and
"The Ghost," the plot is important. Indeed, with a taste
for conundrums, Paulding in these four tales may have
discovered the detective plot later perfected by Poe. In
the first two, circumstantial evidence is prominent; a mystery is stated and solved; the interest lies primarily in
the solution, though the function of detective is not cen-
tered in one person. But "Cobus Yerks" and "The
Ghost," like a typical detective story, pause at the center.
The second part bends back over the first part and explains
it in detail. Of course, this device is as old as the *Odyssey.*
Now the detective intelligence in "Cobus Yerks" is the
Englishman, and in "The Ghost" it is the ghost himself.
In the second, however, a change in the time and setting
weakens the plot. Paulding's passion for explaining things
would tend to lead him into this type of story.

The White Indian is a misanthropic outcast, hiding in a cave, but once he was a happy Dutch boy, competing with an adopted brother for the love of an adopted sister. His brother, in order to win, succeeded in implicating his opponent in a murder charge that resulted in conviction on circumstantial evidence. The White Indian escaped and fled to the wilderness. Years later, hearing that his brother had married the girl and inherited his own estate, he returned home, seeking vengeance. But, coming upon three or four innocent children of his adopted brother and sister, he became compassionate, and abandoned his purpose. This tale, written in the first person, faithfully pictures Dutch love of children and the practice of adopting orphans even when the parents had children of their own. The story, really a condensed novel, begins slowly but ends swiftly and strongly.

7. Another class includes historical stories and tragedies. Among the former are ".Old Times in the New World," which is a mildly humorous account of the Jamestown settlement, and the pleasant allegories, "The History of Uncle Sam and his Boys" and "The History of Uncle Sam and his Womankind." Capable of comedy, Paulding could also write tragedy. His tales, "The White Indian," "The Dumb Girl," and "The Mother's Choice," are brief tragedies of unwise or misdirected love. In the last, the mother victimized her daughter by inducing her to marry a fashionable dandy instead of a young man whom she really loved and wished to marry. The theme of this story is of enduring interest.

8. Contrary to his own theory of fiction, Paulding treated the supernatural in ghost stories and fairy tales. Of the former the best are "The Ghost" and "Cobus Yerks." Though the author grew up with a healthy fear of ghosts, he used them in his stories only when he could

satisfactorily explain them. "The Ghost" is the story of
the exploits of William Morgan, a seaman on a frigate of
the United States about 1800. He is accurately described—
tall, pale, mysterious, with sepulchral voice; he had trances
and sometimes appeared dead. During an alarm of fire he
jumped overboard and was supposed lost. Being an expert
swimmer and a practical joker, he succeeded in getting
back on the frigate unobserved by the 500 sailors. He
then began his ghostly antics, and presently the reader
feels that all the sailors believed in Morgan's ghost. From
port to port, the excitement increased, and he eluded the
most careful searching parties. Some years later the captain met Morgan in Tennessee and got a detailed explanation of the mystery. William Austin's "Peter Rugg, the
Missing Man" is too fantastic for an explanation; but
Paulding's "The Ghost" is rationalized and at least
crudely explained. The tale is decidedly Poesque. The
name of the principal character and the theme of the story
were probably suggested by the anti-masonic excitement
which arose in 1826 over the abduction and supposed murder of William Morgan, a Mason of Batavia, who had
threatened to expose the secrets of the order. His fate
was never positively known, but so much fanatical preju-
dice was aroused against the fraternity that in the election
of 1827 the people forgot party distinctions and supported
or opposed the Masons at the polls.[13]

Satirist, realist, debater, wit, philosopher, politician, and
critic, Paulding yet dearly loved a fairy story. His imagination could create its own wonderland. Here belong
"Cupid and Hymen—an Allegory," "Time and Truth—
an Apologue," "The Little Gold-Fish," "The Magic

[13] Mary L. Booth's *History of the City of New York* (New York,
1880), pp. 731–732; see also J. D. Hammond's *History of Political
Parties in the State of New York*, Vol. 2, Chap. 38 (Albany, 1842).

Spinning Wheel,'' which is probably his best, and a collection entitled *A Gift from Fairyland* (New York, 1838; London, 1840). "The Magic Spinning Wheel" with rural scenes and a fairyland atmosphere inculcates the gospel of work as a cure for human ills.

This classification indicates the general character, range, and probable influence of Paulding's stories. In his letters, his purpose is even more explicit. On the first page of the initial number of the *Southern Literary Messenger* (1834), he thus advised young writers: "Give us something new—something characteristic of your native feelings, and I don't care what it is. I am somewhat tired of licentious love ditties, border legends, affected sorrows, and grumbling misanthropy. I want to see something wholesome, natural, and national." [14] In 1836, as previously shown, he advised Poe to apply his fine humor and abilities "to the faults and foibles of our own people, their peculiarities of habits, and above all to the ridiculous affectations and extravagancies of the fashionable English Literature of the day, which we copy with such admirable success and servility." Though Poe gave little heed to this advice, it appears that he composed *The Narrative of Arthur Gordon Pym* (1838) at Paulding's suggestion after Harpers had declined to publish a volume of Poe's tales.[15] Paulding's stories and satires exemplified his own advice, and probably had more influence on his contemporaries of 1830 than is generally acknowledged.

The main faults in his tales are obvious. As Irving observed, they are such as arise "from hasty and negli-

[14] Letter to T. W. White, *Southern Literary Messenger*, August, 1834.

[15] James A. Harrison's *Life and Letters of Edgar Allan Poe*, Vol. 2, pp. 31–32, and pp. 377–378 (Crowell).

gent composition'': an occasional error in grammar, a
loose sentence, a makeshift plot, an inconsistency in character, dull matter, discursiveness, or an unhappy mingling
of comic and serious elements. But no author is perfect,
and Paulding's extempore method promoted ease and nat-
uralness.

On the other hand, his tales have distinct merits. Most
of them are realistic, wholesome, and natural. They are
usually brief and original. At his best the style is simple,
easy, and direct; the dialogue is often brilliant, easily surpassing Irving's. The tales are free from romantic extravagance and sentimentality, and exhibit a sturdy viril-
ity and a fine sense of human values. Paulding vitalized
the tale and increased its range; he introduced a large
intellectual element—wit, satire, and reflection. His purpose was not only to instruct but to entertain. His method
was primarily comic; he often became a laughing philosopher. Hence, his tales are free from Hawthorne's gloom
and Poe's melancholy. Hawthorne saw life whole but
through a glass somewhat darkly; Poe moved in a shadow
land of lost loves and regrets; but Paulding loved sun-
shine, clear heads, warm hearts, and the great human experiment called life. For Poe, life was a painful mystery;
for Hawthorne, it was a purgatorial experience; for Paulding, the diverting adventure of a serenely self-reliant
soul.

PAULDING'S TALES CHRONOLOGICALLY ARRANGED

(Titles for numbers 7 and 8 have been supplied. The more important tales are starred.)

1807   1. Mine Uncle John, *Salmagundi I,* 1807. A reminiscent character sketch.

1813   * 2. Cupid and Hymen, An Allegory, *The Analectic
Magazine,* Vol. II, 1813.

1814   3. Walbridge, same, January, 1814. Partly autobi-
           ographic, partly fictitious.
        4. The Lost Traveller, same, August, 1814. A story
           of pioneer life.
1815   5. The Adventures of Henry Bird, same, October,
           1815. Simple frontier narrative.
1818   6. *The Backwoodsman: A Poem*, book, New York,
           1818. A long narrative in heroic couplets.
1819 * 7. [Sketch of an Old Dutchman], *Salmagundi II*,
           October, 1819. Humorous account of a real Dutch-
           man (Henry Brevoort, Sr.).
1820 * 8. [Visit of an Indian Chief to Europe], same, July
           and August, 1820. Loose humorous narrative.
        9. The Bashaw of Cyprus, same, August, 1820.
           Sketch of an Eastern character.
1826   10. The Eve of St. John, *The Atlantic Souvenir*, 1826.
           An Eastern love tale. This was the initial article
           in the first American annual.
       11. A Tale of Mystery, same, 1826. A fashionable lady
           mistakes Mr. Stump for Lord Byron.
       12. The Spanish Girl of the Cordilleras, same, 1826.
           Love story placed in South America.
1827 *13. The White Indian, same, 1827. Tale of the New
           York Dutch.
      *14. The Little Dutch Sentinel of the Manhadoes, same,
           1827. A love story with explained ghosts.
1828   15. The Poet's Tale, same, 1828. A loose, unequal
           satire on the rage for Moore's and Byron's poetry.
      *16. Cobus Yerks, same, 1828. Probably the author's
           best short story.
      *17. Un Fainéant (A Loafer), *New York Mirror*, Nov.
           29, 1828. A realistic tale.
1829   18. Benhadar, *The Atlantic Souvenir*, 1829. Painful
           eastern tale of no consequence.
      *19. The Ghost, same, 1830; also in *New York Mirror*,
           Oct. 17, 1829. A ghost story at sea.
      *20, * 21, * 22, 23. *Tales of The Good Woman*, 1829,
           containing The Yankee Roué, The Drunkard, Dys-
           pepsy, and Old Times in the New World. A vol-
           ume of tales.

1830 * 24, * 25, * 26. *Chronicles of the City of Gotham,*
        1830, containing The Azure Hose, The Politician,
        and The Dumb Girl. A volume of tales.

     27. The Angel of Time, *New York Mirror,* August 21,
        1830. Very brief narrative.

     28. The Eve of St. Andrew, same, October 23, 1830;
        republished from *The Atlantic Souvenir* for 1831.
        A realistic story of the western Indians.

  * 29. Legend of the Ancient Tile-roofed Cottage, *New
        York Mirror,* Nov. 20, 1830. A humorous tale of
        a Dutch family.

1831 * 30. Knickerbocker Hall, or The Origin of Baker's
        Dozen, same, Jan. 1, 1831. A Dutch story.

     31. A Trip to Paris, same, Jan. 15, 1831. Humorous
        sketch belittling European attractions.

     32. Want of Excitement, or a Trip to London, same,
        January, 1831. Mostly good talk.

     33. The Malapropos, same, January 22, 1831. Loose
        tale with spirited dialogue.

  * 34. The History of Uncle Sam and His Boys—A Tale
        for Politicians, same, Feb. 19, 1831. An amusing
        allegory of internal improvements.

  * 35. The Victim of Trifles, same, March 12, 1831. A
        pleasant realistic story.

  * 36. Old 76, or The Mysterious Interloper, same, March
        19, 1831. Humorous story.

     37. The Circle of Human Wishes, same, April 9, 1831.
        A tale of little value.

     38. The Nymph of the Mountain, same, April 16, 1831.
        Uneven and fantastic tale for July 4.

  * 39. Time and Truth—An Apologue, same, April 30,
        1831. Time, swift; Truth, slow; yet, "Truth is
        great and will prevail."

     40. A Legend of St. Nicholas, same, May 14, 1831.
        Fanciful story of the origin of St. Nicholas.

  * 41. Jonathan's Visit to the Celestial Empire, same,
        June 18, 1831. Humorous.

  * 42. The Great Medicine, or The Magic Whiskers, same,
        August 6, 1831. A farce.

  * 43. Manners and Morals—A True Story, same, Sept.
        17, 1831. A triangular love tragedy.

* 44. The Mother's Choice—A Fact, same, Sept. 25, 1831. A good example of story-telling and character-drawing.

45. Haschbasch, The Pearl Diver, same, Oct. 1, 1831. Farcical story of Mahometan world.

* 46. The Revenge of St. Nicholas, same, Dec. 31, 1831. Humorous holiday story.

1832 * 47. The Dunce and the Genius, *The Atlantic Souvenir*, 1832. Satire on Byron's poetry, foolish women, and pert boys.

* 48. Too Fast and Too Slow, *New York Mirror*, March 10, 1832. A satire.

* 49. The History of Uncle Sam and His Womankind, same, July 7, 1832. A lively narrative of contemporary events.

* 50. Day and Night or The Water-Carrier of Damascus, same, Dec. 29, 1832. An eastern tale teaching that the industrious are happiest.

51, 52. Two tales, Childe Roeliffe's Pilgrimage and Selim, published in *Tales of Glauber-Spa* (1832), to which Miss Sedgwick, Bryant, Sands, and Leggett contributed stories. The first is principally a description of scenes along the Hudson and Lake Champlain; the second is an eastern tale.

1833 * 53. Claas Schlaschenschlinger, *New York Mirror*, Feb. 2, 1833. Christmas story of a Dutch boy.

* 54. Running Against Time, *The Knickerbocker*, March, 1833. Satire on a slow man who pretends to be fast.

55. Musa, or the Reformation, *New York Mirror*, July 6, 1833. An unconvincing eastern tale.

56. Adam and Eve, same, Dec. 28, 1833. A scene after the pair left paradise.

1834 * 57. Yankee Pedagogues and Dutch Damsels, same, May 3, 1834.

58. A Story for the Holidays, same, Dec. 27, 1834.

1836 * 59. The Magic Spinning Wheel, *The Token and Atlantic Souvenir*, 1836.

1838 * 60. The School of Reform; A Domestic Tale, *U. S. Magazine and Democratic Review*, March, 1838.

1841   61. The Nameless Old Woman, *New York Mirror,* Jan.
             2 and 9, 1841. A study in avarice.

1843   * 62. The Millionaire: A Tale of the Times, *Graham's
             Magazine,* September, 1843. Slow, realistic tale
             with good dialogue.

1844   * 63. History of a Lion, same, Jan., 1844. Story of an
             impostor.

         64. The Old Skinflint Fairy, and Her Goddaughter,
             same, Feb., 1844. Dull and unconvincing.

        * 65. The Two Clocks, same, June, 1844.

        * 66. Poor Genevieve, same, July, 1844. Story of a rich
             lady's quest for a suitable husband.

         67. Murad the Wise, same, Sept., 1844. Story treat-
             ing the problem of evil.

1845   68. The Blind Fiddler of New Amsterdam, same, Jan.,
             1845. Playful sketch.

1846   * 69. The Mother's Tragedy, same, Feb. and March, 1846.
             A tragic story, real and convincing.

         70. The New Science, or the Village Bewitched, same,
             May, 1846. Tedious story of hypnotism.

         71. The Vroucolacas, same, June, 1846. A Mohamme-
             dan tale.

1847   * 72. Musa; or the Pilgrim of Truth, same, Jan., 1847.
             Study in religion.

        * 73. The Man Whom Everybody Pitied, *Godey's Maga-
             zine and Lady's Book,* January, 1847. An amusing
             story of Jubilee Posey's irrepressible good humor.

         74. Fairy Land and Fairy Lore, same, June, 1847.

1848   75. The Little Gold-Fish, *Graham's Magazine,* Jan.,
             1848. A lengthy fairy tale.

         76. The Double Transformation, same, June, 1848. A
             fairy story.

CHAPTER VI

THE NOVELIST

PAULDING wrote five novels. *Koningsmarke* (1823) presented the colonial Swedes of Delaware. *The Dutchman's Fireside* (1831) celebrated the New York Dutch at the time of the French and Indian Wars. *Westward Ho!* (1832) made Virginia and Kentucky its scene. *The Old Continental* (1846) pictured New York in the Revolution. The last, *The Puritan and His Daughter* (1849), written in the decline of his mental powers, carries the principal characters from Cromwell's England to the colonies. Of these the best are the New York fictions, and next the tale of Kentucky. All were translated into one or more of the European languages.

Paulding's novels exemplify his theory of rational fiction. This theory, derived chiefly from a study of Fielding's practice, was explained in the preceding chapter. From Paulding's essay on "National Literature" (1820) it is desirable to quote here a passage, in which he thus advised the young novelist:

"By freeing himself from a habit of servile imitation; by daring to think and feel, and express his feelings; by dwelling on scenes and events connected with our pride and affections; by indulging in those little peculiarities of thought, feeling, and expression which belong to every nation; by borrowing from nature, and not from those who disfigure or burlesque her, he may and will in time destroy the ascendancy of foreign taste and opinions, and elevate his own in the place of them. . . .

"The favorite, yet almost hopeless object of my old age, is to

93

see this attempt consummated. For this purpose, it is my delight to furnish occasionally such hints as may turn the attention of those who have leisure, health, youth, genius, and opportunities, to domestic subjects on which to exercise their powers. Let them not be disheartened, even should they sink into a temporary oblivion in the outset. This country is not destined to be always behind in the race of literary glory."

Two years later, in a fine passage praising the charm and geniality of Scott, he thus compared him with Fielding and Miss Edgeworth:

"But I cannot help thinking it is placing him where he ought not to be, to put him on a level with Fielding, Smollett, Goldsmith, and Miss Edgeworth. He belongs, I imagine, to a different class of beings; to a class of authors, who, when the charm of novelty expires, and curiosity is satisfied in the development of the story, will never be much relished or sought after for other and more lasting beauties. Of Fielding I think it may be fairly said, that he has produced one of the most consummate works of fiction that ever the world saw. In knowledge of life and human motives; in variety, strength, contrast, and probability of character; in the invention and unequalled skill in arranging his incidents and in the simplicity and perfection of the dénouement of the story, Tom Jones has never, I believe, been surpassed. Smollett is only second, yet a great way off; and Goldsmith, in the delineation of human nature at the domestic fire-side of virtuous simplicity, is yet without an equal. Each of these writers, without going out of the bounds of probability, or offending against 'the modesty of nature,' by extravagant and incongruous events, or boisterous, uncontrolled passion, has produced works, that appeal far more powerfully to the heart and the imagination, than the dashing succession of characters and events, that only hang together by a chain of improbabilities, or by the thread of history, exhibited in the work of the Great Unknown. Miss Edgeworth, among the living novelists, so far as my reading extends, is the only one that has ever heard there was such a thing as human nature, or who is aware that, by the exercise of a chastened judgment, a delicate taste, and a playful wit, ordinary characters and every-day incidents may be invested with charms a thousand times more engaging and interesting, than the monstrous creations, or copies of a Maturin, or even a Great Unknown." [1]

In view of this high praise of Henry Fielding, one would expect Paulding to choose him for his instructor in fiction. In the summer of 1823, he anonymously published *Koningsmarke, The Long Finne, A Story of the New World*, planned and written in imitation of *Tom Jones*. Within two decades the novel was thrice published in England and was translated into German. It is divided into nine books of four or five brief chapters each, the initial chapter of each book being a little humorous or critical essay. Probably the best is in book five.

The scene of the story is the old Swedish settlement in Delaware and among the Indians of central Pennsylvania. The time is about 1660. The first three books with little narrative present a satirical description of Governor Peter Piper's court, subjects, and ecclesisatical system. The hero, charged with an attempt to seduce the people from their allegiance to Gustavus Adolphus of Sweden, is comically tried before the governor and lodged in jail. After winning the favor of Christina, the governor's daughter, the hero (like Paulding's father) is released by the burning of the jail. Soon afterwards a dispute with the Indians over hunting and fishing concessions ends in their burning the town and carrying away eight captives, including the Long Finne and Christina. Several of the captives are killed, but the hero and heroine are adopted by the tribe, both being befriended by Deer Eyes, an Indian maid of the Pocahontas type. After some months the lovers and a white companion escape, but after traveling for a day and killing an Indian, they are recaptured. The two men, tried for desertion and the murder of a chief, are condemned to torture. Then follows the most dramatic action

[1] *A Sketch of Old England*, Vol. II, pp. 149–150.

of the novel. Deer Eyes had rescued Christina, but a
violent crowd of Indians seized the two men, painted them
black with charcoal and grease and fastened them to stakes
in preparation for the horrible ceremony of burning. Deer
Eyes begged in vain for the captives, until a crash of
thunder, loud and sharp, arrested the ceremony and attracted all eyes heavenward as to a supernatural inter-
vention. The Indian maid, taking advantage of the phe-
nomenon, cried out:

"Hark! The Great Spirit bears testimony against this deed.
You heard his voice in the air. It came not from a cloud in the
skies. It is the great Master of Life, that cries out from above
against his people that have offended him. In his name I command you to stop—in his name I command you to spare these
white men!" [2]

Awed by the thunder, the frantic tribe grew calm, and
the chiefs postponed the ceremony until the will of the
Great Spirit could be learned. The next day the priest
howled himself into a frenzy and decided against the white
men. But a group of rescuers sent out by William Penn
opportunely appeared and placated the Indians. So the
lovers returned to Delaware. The last three books are
rather slow and dull, satirizing the settlement. A British
fleet ended the Swedish rule, and carried Long Finne to
New York, where after his release the lovers were reunited
and married.

The novel has the marks of an initial, imitative effort.
It is deficient in unity and cumulative force, and for two
volumes there is too little action. The mood or tone sometimes shifts unnaturally from serious to comic and vice-
versa. The principal white characters, however, have vital
individuality, and the Indians, though somewhat Dutchy

[2] *Koningsmarke*, book 6, chapter 4.

and unskilled as fighters, are convincingly real. The satire on Scott's romances, sordid ministers, and gossipy old ladies would not increase the popularity of the novel. The thunder scene is finely conceived and convincingly written; it presents a dramatic clash of characters and contending interests involving love, hate, revenge, superstition, charity, and reverence for the Great Spirit. The editor of the *New York Mirror* in a discriminating review published in November, 1823, thought that the author might turn out to be another "great unknown."

Though *Kongingsmarke* had some merit and was mildly successful, the author turned to the short story, as shown in the preceding chapter, and did not publish his second novel till eight years later. During these years his life was uneventful, but his mind was active and creative. Brevoort's letters to Irving at this time contain comic notes on Paulding's mode of life; their acidity may be owing to Brevoort's feeling that perhaps Paulding was satirizing such lazy rich men as himself.

In March, 1829, Brevoort thus replied to Irving's inquiries:

"As to Paulding, he continues to lead a sort of Terrapin's life—sometimes when the sun shines he puts forth his head and walks up Broad Way, but there is no use in striving to bring him into habits of social intercourse—they seem to have become irksome to him. Although we live within two hundred yards of each other, we might just as well be separated by so many leagues. He writes Books, but they are the products of a mind at war with everything." [3]

Soon after the satiric *Tales of the Good Woman* was published, Brevoort wrote again: "He has certainly lost the art of writing; he seems to be troubled with a sort of mental dyspepsia, everything turns acid that passes

[3] *Letters of Brevoort to Irving,* Vol. 2, p. 25.

through his mind—and yet Paulding is a man of genius.'' [4]
Such compliments ''a man of genius'' received because he
had enough courage and insight to satirize evils in society.
In the same year, however, Brevoort recorded that Paulding had just entertained at dinner all his old friends,
including Governor Johnston, and that they had drunk to
Irving's health and prosperity.[5]

As a matter of fact, at this time Paulding was doing his
best work. By January, 1830, he had completed his principal novel, *The Dutchman's Fireside,* for which Harpers
paid $1400; and he had gained a prize of $300 offered by
James H. Hackett for the best original comedy with an
American as the leading character. Paulding's play, *The
Lion of the West,* was selected by a committee consisting
of W. C. Bryant, Fitz-Greene Halleck, and Prosper M.
Wetmore. After this two-fold success, Paulding for several years shared popular honors with Irving and Cooper.
He was subjected to the acid test of praise and popularity.
His tales and novels were in demand; even his old enemy,
England, was gracious enough to read and commend them.
For Paulding it was a happy time, and he continued to
write with unusual speed and effectiveness—sketches, tales,
another novel, and a life of Washington. By 1833 Harpers felt justified in beginning a collected edition of his
works, which included so much inferior or forgotten political and journalistic matter as to provoke N. P. Willis's
ungenerous criticism in *The Corsair.* (See *Southern Literary Messenger,* Vol. 5, pp. 415–417.)

The Lion of the West, played in England under the
title ''A Kentuckian's Trip to New York in 1815,'' has
apparently been lost. In the principal cities of the United
States Mr. Hackett presented the play successfully for

4 Same, Vol. 2, p. 38.
5 Same, Vol. 2, p. 43.

twenty years, and it ran for several weeks in two London theaters. An English critic thus describes the character of Nimrod Wildfire:

"He may be compared to an open-hearted, childish giant, whom any one might deceive but none could daunt. His whimsical extravagance of speech arises from a mere exuberance of animal spirits; and his ignorance of the conventional restraints of society he overbalances by a heart that would scorn to do a mean or dishonest action." [6]

Early in June, 1832, Lieutenant E. T. Coke of the British army attended a performance in Philadelphia. It delighted the audience, he says, though he thought that much of the dialogue was in an unintelligible idiom; he also observes that the play had so incensed some Westerners that they made threats against Mr. Hackett.[7]

The Lion of the West demonstrated Paulding's skill in dialogue and in comedy. His fiction of this period had much good talk, and some of his stories were related in the 'first person. His earlier play, "The Bucktails; or, Americans in England," which was written soon after the War of 1812, but probably revised before publication in *American Comedies* in 1847, is a five-act prose comedy with echoes from Shakespeare. The scene is in England. Of the main characters, Henry and Frank Tudor and Jane Warfield are Americans; and the Obsolete family and Lord Noland, the villain, are British. Parts of the comedy satirize the English king and the nobility. Besides two pretty love scenes, the chief complication arises from Noland's abduction of Jane Warfield, an American heiress. At one point the feeling rises to the dignity of blank verse. The play is both readable and actable.

Paulding's second and best novel, *The Dutchman's Fire-*

[6] *Literary Life of J. K. Paulding*, pp. 218–220.
[7] *A Subaltern's Furlough*, etc., Vol. 1, p. 35 (New York, 1833).

side (1831), recommended to an English publisher by Bulwer Lytton and so popular that it was translated into five European languages, builds itself around the adventures of a Dutch boy and girl. With many lines of interest it made a deep impression on contemporary readers.

"This Tale," [wrote an English reviewer] "is an exception to tales in general, and is as much worth reading for its style, its moral remarks, and veracious descriptions, as for the interest of the narrative, the striking character of its personages, but above all, for its correct and spirited views of Red-Indian manners and morals." [8]

Commending the author's humor and power of philosophical analysis, George P. Morris observed: "To us he seems not inferior in the extent and diversity of his talents, to any American writer of the present school. There is a keen insight into the human character and human motives." [9]

This novel is a veracious account of the New York Dutch before the Revolution. The physical center of the story is near Albany, in a Dutch farm mansion built of imported bricks and situated a little way from the Hudson in a rich meadow carpeted with "delicious green." On the estate three Vancour brothers lived in peace and plenty. Into their circle came the capricious Catalina Vancour from a New York boarding school, and bashful Sybrandt Westbrook, an adopted son, from his secluded studies under the local Domine. Secretly admiring the girl and seeing her bestow her favors on an English Colonel, Sybrandt resolved to divert himself by going on a trading trip to the Indians. Among them he met the famous Indian Commissioner, Sir William Johnson, who exerted a powerful influence over the timid youth and eventually transformed him into a

8 *The Westminster Review*, October, 1831; Vol. 15, p. 495.
9 *New York Mirror*, June 4, 1831.

man of action. After several distressing episodes with a
"civilized" Indian, Catalina transferred the scene to
fashionable New York. Next, Sybrandt was carried by the
stirring events of the French and Indian Wars to the
fighting near Lake Champlain; and after a dramatic complication near the end the love action culminated in mingled
joy and sorrow.

Though the plot gets off in leisurely Dutch fashion and
sags somewhat at the satiric middle, it pulls itself together
for a dramatic finish. Containing little action, the early
chapters present Dutch character sketches, poetical descriptions, and wise reflections. Still imitating Fielding, the
author made his chapters brief, but discarded book divis-
ions with introductory essays. The psychology of the
novel reminds one of Hawthorne, but its adventure recalls
Cooper.

The principal character is Sybrandt Westbrook, an
orphan son of a Dutch beauty and a British officer, adopted
by Dennis Vancour and educated at home by Domine
Stettinius in a primitive Dutch manner. By nineteen, the
boy was a scholar, but also a "shy, awkward, reserved, abstract being," adoring woman yet afraid of her, fearful of
trifles yet fearless in great perils, feeling awkward and
imagining himself ridiculed. Under this impression he became miserable. By a series of vicissitudes, however, his
character and will power were developed; and, aided by
the advice and example of Sir William Johnson, he became
confident and masterful. He is a developing character.
Sybrandt's youth resembles Paulding's in so many respects, and Johnson's influence over Sybrandt so parallels
William Irving's over Paulding that the novel has autobiographic interest. Many of the complications grow out
of the hero's painful timidity developed in seclusion.
Catalina, fresh from a New York boarding school and city

society, is a wholesome girl but somewhat capricious.
When mastered by a genuine love, she too is remade into
a self-reliant, trustworthy woman. Near the end, a report
of Sybrandt's death draws this picture of her from
Paulding:

"She did not faint—she did not shriek, or scream, or wring her
hands—but she sat like a statue of pure white marble carved
by some famous artist to represent the silence of unutterable
grief." [10]

Of the remaining characters, Sir William Johnson
(1715–1774) is the most forceful and best drawn; indeed,
he is a powerful figure, cowing drunken Indians and out-
witting the chiefs in diplomatic parley. Other distinctive
characters are the sober Dennis and the volatile Ariel Vancour; the Irish Gilfillan, who had rather die than lose a
dancing leg; Mrs. Vancour and Mrs. Aubineau with their
love of titles and scarlet uniforms; a Dutch river captain,
who believed in making haste slowly; Timothy Weasel, a
sort of embittered Hawkeye; and two Indians, both
treacherous and cruel.

An excellent supplement and a better novel is Cooper's
Satanstoe (1845). Though the stories relate to the same
period, each presents a different phase. Paulding paints
the Hudson in summer; Cooper, in winter. Paulding
stresses country life; Cooper, the cities of New York and
Albany. Paulding emphasizes character development;
Cooper is best in adventure. Paulding's main characters
excepting Johnson and Sybrandt are pure Dutch; Cooper's
are mixed with the English. Paulding had a firmer grip
on Dutch life; Cooper's Dutchmen do not even talk consistently. Paulding's prose, restrained and succinct, ac-

[10] *The Dutchman's Fireside*, p. 346 (1868).

complished nearly as much in one hundred thousand words as Cooper's easy prolixity in twice the number. Yet *Satanstoe* is one of Cooper's best stories—realistic and charming. *The Dutchman's Fireside* (1831) at least anticipated, if it did not influence, *Satanstoe* (1845) in these particulars; the scene of both novels is Albany and its neighborhood; both dwell upon Dutch domestic manners; in both, the hero rescues the heroine from death in the Hudson River; in both, the hero joins the unsuccessful expedition of the English forces to Ticonderoga; and both authors acknowledge their indebtedness to Mrs. Anne M. Grant's *Memoirs of an American Lady* (1808), which is a graphic record of her observations at Albany before the Revolution.

In May, 1832, Washington Irving in "a tumult of enjoyment" returned to New York after a long pilgrimage of seventeen years in Europe. On May 30, three hundred banqueters greeted him at the City Hotel. Chancellor Kent presided, and on Irving's right sat his old friend and literary associate, James K. Paulding, whose simple toast was "Old Times, old friends, and old associations." [11] In July, Irving, Paulding, and some of their friends, joining an exodus from the city, retreated to West Point and thence made a brief excursion to the Catskill Mountains.[12]

Meanwhile, by April, 1832, Paulding had placed with Harpers a third novel, *Westward Ho!* for which he received $1500. In October the first edition of 5000 copies attested the confidence of the publishers in the novel. The delay in publication was probably owing to the epidemic of cholera asphyxia which struck the city in June, and by the

[11] *New York Mirror*, June 9, 1832.
[12] *Olde Ulster, An Historical and Genealogical Magazine*, Jan.–Dec., 1905 (Kingston, N. Y.), Vol. 1, pp. 8–9 (Copy in New York Public Library).

middle of August carried 2600 to their graves and scattered one-third of the 220,000 inhabitants in every direction.[13]

Westward Ho! is the story of a prominent family that removed from Virginia to the "dark and bloody ground" of Kentucky. The early chapters depict "Colonel" Cuthbert Dangerfield's hospitality in the Old Dominion, and his unfortunate ventures, which ended in a losing bet on a favorite race horse. Compelled to pay his debts, he sold his estate. With a snug balance of 5000 pounds, and his wife, children, and a slave or two, he set out for Kentucky to found Dangerfieldville. On the way he met Bushfield, an experienced frontiersman, who guided and counseled them. In time the son went to college, and the daughter, Virginia, became attached to a mysterious newcomer, Dudley Rainsford, whose fear of an impending doom and display of religious frenzy are revealed and ultimately cured in the second half of the novel. "The moral of our tale," the author concludes, "will, we trust be found in the warning it holds against the approaches of fanaticism, the weak indulgence of presentiments of evil," and also in the wisdom "of a solid, permanent reliance on the goodness of Providence."

Though the novel begins as a story of adventure, it develops into an unpleasant psychological study, shifting its emphasis from the outer to the inner world. Consequently, it suffers from too much introspection and too little action, and reveals the author's literary kinship with Hawthorne. However, by learning to overcome obstacles vigorously, Colonel Dangerfield developed his better qualities, and without loss of charity became decisive and efficient. Virginia's tenderness, devotion, and faith ultimately restored her lover to mental health and useful

13 Dr. J. W. Francis in *New York Mirror*, Sept. 1, 1832.

activity. The grandiloquent Bushfield, resembling Nimrod Wildfire in *The Lion of the West*, is an original character. The Colonel's sixteenth cousin, Ulysses Littlejohn, is perennially interesting. The negroes are natural and in their way attractive. In broken English a Frenchman becomes a mouthpiece for some of Paulding's notions. Among the minor characters imperfectly sketched are an Indian and an Englishman. Of Virginia life the author had considerable first-hand knowledge, but for the Kentucky frontier he borrowed freely from Rev. Timothy Flint's *Recollections of the Last Ten Years Passed in the Valley of the Mississippi* (1826).

In 1833 and 1834 Paulding published nothing except a few stories in the *New York Mirror*. He was preparing *A Life of Washington*, which was issued by Harper and Brothers in 1835, and which was so well received that nine American editions were called for before it was overshadowed by Irving's life of our first president. The next year he published a social study, *Slavery in the United States*, and about the same time *The Book of Saint Nicholas*, a collection of ten stories previously printed, except one, in periodical form. On March 30, 1837, Irving, Paulding, Halleck, Poe, Bryant, and other distinguished gentlemen were entertained at the City Hotel by the booksellers of New York City. In May, 1838, after some hesitation, Paulding accepted President Van Buren's invitation to become Secretary of the Navy. In a letter to Irving about this time, he gave potent reasons for his habit of writing for newspapers:

"If men of good principles, [he reasoned] keep aloof from all participation in newspapers, they will naturally fall into the hands of interested, factious, and unprincipled demagogues, and become sheer instruments of mischief. In no other country has the daily press such a wide influence, and I don't know what will

become of us if that influence is directed by men without talent
or principles." [14]

In the next decade after leaving his cabinet position
in March, 1841, Paulding wrote two more novels. The
first was *The Old Continental: or the Price of Liberty*
(1846). Substantially written several years before and
revised before publication, the work is more finished than
Westward Ho! It is probably his second best novel. In
a preface, he states that his purpose was to present a
domestic picture of the Revolutionary War in New York.
The scene is the east bank of the Hudson between the
Highlands and Manhattan Island, the so-called "no man's
land" of the Revolution, which some wit declared had
neither law nor gospel.

In the novel a youth called John (really John Paulding),
left with his grandparents by his father, a captain in the
Revolutionary army, determined to volunteer in the
patriot army in order to serve his country and to win the
favor of the Old Continental, Col. Hammond, father of his
sweetheart, Jane Hammond. So John succeeded in joining
his father's company in the Highlands. The following
winter he overheard and threatened to expose the plot of
several mutinous soldiers, who tried to clear themselves
by falsely accusing the youth. In a dramatic manner he
barely escaped execution as a traitor. Immediately afterwards he secured leave of absence to repair his reputation
in the eyes of Col. Hammond and his daughter. Later,
while serving as a trusted spy, John was captured and imprisoned by the British. Meanwhile it was rumored that
he had deserted to the British. To learn the truth, Col.
Hammond in his old British uniform, accompanied by his
colored servant, went on a delightful Don Quixote journey

[14] *Literary Life*, pp. 262–263.

to the American headquarters, where under a pledge of secrecy he learned the facts. After a time in the New York prison, John contrived to escape and eluded the guards, but above the city he was recaptured, and consigned to a foul and pestilential prison ship. There he was surprised to find his emaciated and dying father. Cleverly winning the admiration and confidence of his guards, John secured certain liberties about the ship, and one evening while amusing his captors, he suddenly jumped overboard and escaped to Long Island. After several bloody episodes with outlaws and further complications, the hero with his two comrades captured Major André, and in the end received the nation's thanks and Col. Hammond's daughter.

Had Paulding maintained the pace that he set in the earlier portions of the story, *The Old Continental* would be his best novel. As it stands, it is a memorable narrative, depicting the neutral ground more truly than did Cooper's *The Spy*. The author had become seasoned; he had digested and mastered his materials; he wrote with ease and persuasiveness. Action, scene, characters, dialogue, humor, love of nature, and knowledge of life are successfully fused together.

Whether the reader is smiling at Col. Hammond's little tyrannies, or observing intoxicated and mutinous soldiers in a winter hut, or patriot prisoners in the infamous prison ships, or a Presbyterian wife converting her Quaker husband to the American cause—he is held by the author's tale of adventure and by his truthful and picturesque portrayal of the characters.

Towards the end, however, some of the incidents are trite and unnecessary, and some of the dialogue is cheap and superfluous. The capture of André, instead of being the most dramatic incident, becomes a trivial affair, dissipating the reader's interest. At this point Paulding's imagination failed him. The empty vaporings of the half-witted Hagar Raven are poor substitutes for a clear and vigorous exposition of the disaster then impending over the American cause.

But Paulding was not aspiring to the dignity of historical romance. "The design was," he wrote in the preface, "to convey to the mind of the reader some idea of the spirit, the sufferings, and the sacrifices of a class of people who are seldom, if ever, individualized in history." He goes on to say that the hero actually existed and that many of the incidents really happened. Famous characters he purposely omitted or minimized. His claims are so modest as to disarm the critic. The style is uniformly good and firm and enlivened by a suffused humor. The dialogue is abundant and usually pertinent.

The original of the hero was John Paulding (1758–1818), a native of Westchester and a first cousin of the author. The hero's father served in the Revolution. John was a brave, handsome fellow, six feet tall. Thrice he was captured and imprisoned by the British, and twice he escaped. After the war he settled on the farm given him by New York state; and, to establish his courage, patriotism, and winsomeness beyond controversy, he married three times and fathered nineteen children, one of whom, Hiram, became an admiral in the American navy.[15] According to Mr. Edgar M. Bacon of Tarrytown, Col. Hammond should probably be identified with Col. James Hammond, a picturesque patriot, the hero of several unusual incidents, and a trusted agent of Washington, who was nearly captured at Col. Hammond's house in Tarrytown.

The last and least successful of Paulding's novels, *The Puritan and His Daughter* (1849), gives many indications

---

[15] M. D. Raymond's *Souvenir of the Revolutionary Soldiers' Monument Dedication at Tarrytown*, New York (1894), pp. 155–161.

JOHN PAULDING (1758–1818)

One of André's Captors, the Hero of *The Old Continental*, and First Cousin of the Author.

From a print in the New York Public Library.

of a decline of his mental powers. Strangely enough, this child of his old age was his favorite. Its defects are clearly indicated by the manner of composition. In December, 1848, he thus wrote to a friend:

"I have undertaken to splice the 'Puritan's Daughter,' as they do steamboats, by cutting them in two, and putting a piece in the middle. With dove-tailing here a little, loitering by the way, and stopping now and then to have a talk like Cooper, I shall be able to stretch it to the proper dimensions [two volumes], I hope, without doing it much damage." [16]

Consequently, the novel is loose, rambling, and as a whole ineffective. The story begins in Cromwell's England, shifts to Virginia for most of the incidents, then to New England, and finally to an undefined place apparently in the Mississippi Valley. The principal characters are Harold Habington and his daughter Miriam, for whom the novel is named. The story has a mild interest, a vein of humor and satire, and frequent descriptions. The incidents involving the Puritan, a Virginia Cavalier, and the romance of their children are the best. Hostile Indians appear; and the heroine, charged with witchcraft, nearly loses her life. At the end the author stated that his purpose was to inculcate piety instead of bigotry, and the healing balm of religion instead of the venom of sectarianism.

Though Paulding read both Scott and Cooper with pleasure, and though he was probably influenced by them, yet in his novels he was in large measure independent of current fashions in fiction. For models he reverted to Henry Fielding and Oliver Goldsmith. His attitude toward Scott somewhat resembled that of Fielding toward Richardson. In a romantic and sentimental age, Paulding was a realist. Since his tendency to satirize and philoso-

16 Quoted in *Literary Life*, p. 313.

phize detracted from his ability as a narrator, his novels
are somewhat deficient in action. His plots are simply and
plainly constructed. In exposition and argument he had
native ability, but he learned to tell a story only after long
and arduous practice. Hence, he was more successful in
the delineation of character, as shown by the portraits in
the *The Dutchman's Fireside*. His dialogue is usually
natural and character-revealing. As a novelist, he is at
his best in presenting the New York Dutch. Beautiful
threads in his fiction are the bits of philosophy and the
poetical descriptions of nature. He is witty rather than
sentimental; realistic rather than romantic; and to adventure he adds a psychological interest.

CHAPTER VII

CRITIC AND POET

"BEFORE we have an American literature," wrote Lowell in his essay on Poe in 1845, "we must have an American criticism." That is true, but in reality every worthy author is either an active or a potential critic. When Cooper boasted that he could compose a better novel than the one he was reading, he was exercising the critical faculty. The creative writer is like a good architect; by acquiring a comprehensive and digested knowledge of what has been accomplished in his special field, he is fitted to conceive and execute a new work in accordance with the fundamental laws of his art. From the known and tested he advances to the unknown and original.

Though Paulding was neither a regular nor a systematic critic, he put forth between 1815 and 1836 a small body of social and literary criticism. This material colors some of his tales and novels, and seasons a dozen volumes, principally *Letters from the South, A Sketch of Old England, Salmagundi* (Second Series), *A Life of Washington,* and *Slavery in the United States.* A thinker and a prolific writer, he treated nearly every phase of American life— foreign relations, politics, religion, slavery, national growth, industry, wealth, theories of prose and poetry, and contemporary authors. For this work his principal qualifications were his wide reading, independent thought, and Dutch common sense. That he had considerable ability in coining effective aphorisms is shown by the following:

111

"High rents and heavy taxes will spoil even paradise."

"The happiness of the people at large is the end of all good government."

"Declamation is a good prop to error; but facts are the best support of truth."

"It is better to be a good imitator of Milton than an original Lord Byron."

The following passage is typical of his social criticism:

"I shall never forget how the good alderman, your father, dropt his knife and fork, one day, when I asserted at his table, that ———— the great merchant, who was actually president of a bank, and had the credit of being worth millions, was, in feeling, intellect, and action, no better than a pedlar. The alderman looked at me as if I had abused General Washington or the Bible; and I have never sat at the good man's table since. But without exactly quarrelling with that sordid disposition, or that ostentatious, yet vulgar profusion, which in general actuates the people of our great cities, to the exclusion of every nobler pursuit, and all rational economy; still I may venture to lament its universality. In days of yore, Plutus, although he shone in gold and precious stones, hid himself in the bowels of the earth; but now he is seen clothed in ragged bank-notes, taking precedence every where in the city drawing-rooms. There is now no place where a knot of harmless people of moderate fortune can sit down in the undisturbed enjoyment of social ease, or the cultivation of literature and science, free from the intrusion of tobacco, tar, pitch, potash, and cod-fish; sandahs, baftas, bugli-poors, and all the jargon of East India commodities. If they have a moderate competency, they are beset by greedy beggars, who, by dint of perseverance, at length tempt them to engage in some profitable speculation, which draws them gradually from their former pursuits, and ingulphs them for ever in the vortex of gain." [1]

Paulding's Americanism knew no narrow or sectional bounds. Though in early life he had regarded southerners lightly, after an acquaintance with them he praised and

[1] *Letters from the South*, Vol. I, pp. 50–52.

commended them. He admired the stability, industry, sobriety, and economy of the Dutch and Quakers; yet he felt they were unambitious in the pursuit of knowledge. Though too realistic as an author to be very popular with the ladies, he judged them sanely. At Berkeley Springs he observed these types: the sentimental lady; the blue stocking who is all for literature; the invincible belle who goes about seeking whom she may devour; the piously scandalous matron; the major general who marshals her daughters or nieces for Cupid's battle; and the home-maker who finds her happiness in the domestic virtues.[2]

Like Wordsworth and Coleridge, Paulding was both reverent and critical of the church. Since he believed there is "a natural religious feeling pervading the whole human race" and expressing itself in some form of worship, he rejected the teaching of the alleged depravity and infidelity of mankind. Like Luther, he was impatient of a servile obedience to church domination, and he could see no disharmony between true religion and innocent amusements, including the theater and sports. He believed that God intended people to be happy. While he revered a minister who practiced what he preached as an ambassador of heaven, he recognized no obligation to bow the knees of his understanding "to every young gentleman in spectacles and a black coat."[3]

The difficulty an Indian experienced in trying to choose a Christian denomination is thus set forth:

"Brother, you say your religion is the only true religion in the world. Good. I have been in Canada, and there they told me theirs was the only true religion. Good. I have been at Boston, where they assured me the religion of the people of Canada

2 Same, Vol. 2, p. 230.
3 Same, Vol. 2, pp. 139–142.

was the religion of the bad spirit, and that theirs was the only true one. Good. I have been at the Manhattans, where they called the white people of Boston bad people, and said that they had no religion. Good. I have been at Coaquanock, among the Big Hats, and they told me the religion of the Manhattans was not the right sort. Good. I am here, and you say, brother, ours is the only good religion, and you must believe like me. Good. But brother, which am I to believe? You say, all of you, that the good book out of which you preach is what you all take for your guide, and that it is written by the Great Spirit himself, yet you all differ among yourselves. Now, brother, hear what I have got to say. As soon as you shall agree among yourselves which is the true religion, I shall think of joining you. Good." [4]

In several volumes the dominant element is social criticism. *The Merry Tales of the Three Wise Men of Gotham* (1826) is a misnamed volume, for the narrative is so slight that the pieces in the collection should not be called tales. They are really narrative essays. In the first, a humorous exposition, Paulding satirized Robert Owen's idea of the perfectibility of man. The second is a pleasant satire on courts and laws. The third, called "The Perfection of Science," belittles the pretentions of phrenology. These papers present Paulding as a conservative student of life without romantic delusions or impossible dreams. *The New Mirror for Travellers* (1828), a satire on fashionable summer resorts, was so hasty and inconsequential that it may be passed without comment.

By 1835 the subject of slavery was assuming such alarming importance and so seriously threatening the dissolution of the Union that Paulding was impelled to write an apology, called *Slavery in the United States*. The difficulties of his task he fully appreciated, for he knew that "almost every argument in mitigation of the atrocity of slavery," as he wrote to a friend, "goes directly in the teeth of the

[4] *Koningsmarke*, Vol. 1, pp. 199–200.

fundamental principles of our government.'' But his main bulwark, later Lincoln's, was that no national evil could be greater than the dissolution of the Union. His main arguments were that slavery was recognized in the Bible; that originally slaves were captives who had saved their lives by yielding liberty; that emancipation would produce more misery and misgovernment than it would assuage; that property rights in slaves were as defensible as the land rights that the English wrested from the Indians; that the slavery laws were humane and considerate; that the slaves were better off than some northern factory workers, or many British laborers, or the European peasants; and finally that the Abolitionists were fanatical. In defence of Paulding's reasoning we should remember that both in New York and in Virginia he had observed slavery in its most attractive aspects, and that most of his arguments were already hoary with age. The book, written in an easy, deliberate manner, shows the author's ability in close reasoning and in making a plausible case out of intractable material.

His two-volume life of Washington ranks high among early American biographies. By 1858 it had passed through ten editions. In its preparation the author made considerable research over a period of years; from reliable persons who had known Washington he collected first-hand information. Though Paulding's manner is quiet, unpretentious, and effective, the book is probably too eulogistic for modern readers. But the author was writing for young people, and he felt that the public and private virtues of Washington were eminently worthy of imitation. Paulding's biography drew high praise from Edgar Allan Poe.

"We have read, [Poe wrote] Mr. Paulding's 'Life of Washington' with a degree of interest seldom excited in us by the perusal of any book whatever. We are convinced by a deliberate examination of the design, manner, and rich material of the work, that, as it grows in age, it will grow in the estimation of our countrymen, and, finally, will not fail to take a deeper hold upon the public mind, and upon the public affections, than any work upon the same subject, or of a similar nature, which has been yet written—or, possibly, which may be written hereafter. Indeed, we cannot perceive the necessity of anything farther upon the great theme of Washington. Mr. Paulding has completely and most beautifully filled the vacuum which the works of Marshall and Sparks have left open. He has painted the boy, the man, the husband, and the Christian. He has introduced us to the private affections, aspirations, and charities of that hero whose affections of all affections were the most serene, whose aspirations the most god-like, and whose charities the most gentle and pure. He has taken us abroad with the patriot-farmer in his rambles about his homestead. He has seated us in his study and shown us the warrior-Christian in unobtrusive communion with his God. He has done all this too, and more, in a simple and quiet manner, in a manner peculiarly his own, and which, mainly because it is his own, cannot fail to be exceedingly effective. Yet it is very possible that the public may, for many years to come, overlook the rare merits of a work whose want of arrogant assumption is so little in keeping with the usages of the day, and whose striking simplicity and *naïveté* of manner give, to a cursory examination, so little evidence of the labor of composition. We have no fears, however, for the future. Such books as these before us go down to posterity like rich wines, with a certainty of being more valued as they go. They force themselves, with the gradual but rapidly accumulating power of strong wedges, into the hearts and understandings of a community.

"In regard to the style of Mr. Paulding's 'Washington,' it would scarcely be doing it justice to speak of it merely as well adapted to its subject and to its immediate design. Perhaps a rigorous examination would detect an occasional want of euphony and some inaccuracies of syntactical arrangement. But nothing could be more out of place than any such examination in respect to a book whose forcible, rich, vivid, and comprehensive English might advantageously be held up as a model for the young writers of the land. There is no better literary manner than the manner of Mr. Paulding. Certainly no American, and possibly no living writer of England, has more of those numerous peculiarities which go to the formation of a happy style. It is questionable, we think, whether any writer of any country combines as many of these peculiarities with as much of that essential negative virtue, the absence of affectation. We repeat, as our confident opinion, that it would be difficult, even with great care and labor, to improve upon the general manner of the volumes now before us, and that they contain many long individual passages of a force and beauty not to be surpassed by the finest passages of the finest writers in any time or country. It is this striking character in the 'Washington' of Mr. Paulding —striking and peculiar indeed at a season when we are so culpably inattentive to all matters of this nature as to mistake for style the fine airs at second hand of the silliest romancers —it is this character, we say, which should insure the fulfillment of the writer's principal design, in the immediate introduction of his book into every respectable academy in the land." [5]

The two preceding chapters treat Paulding's conception of fiction. Most of his literary criticism in other fields is found in *A Sketch of Old England* (1822), in the introductory chapter to each book of *Koningsmarke* (1823), in his fiction, and in his magazine articles.

Of American prose he wrote in 1817:

"It appears to me that a great portion of our prose writers have also lost sight of nature and simplicity, and deviated into the same faults that characterize so much of our poetry. This unnatural and inflated style of writing abounds, not only in those productions which admit of greater latitude of declamation, but what is quite ridiculous, obtrudes itself in the sober declarations of public bodies; the addresses of plain homespun manufacturing societies; and not unfrequently may be detected in advertisements of farms and runaway negroes. If a ship is launched now-a-days, she must needs 'glide majestically to her destined element';—everything is swelled to an unnatural expansion on paper. Schools, where A, B, C, is taught, have become Acade-

[5] Edgar Allan Poe's *Marginalia*, originally published in *Southern Literary Messenger* (1835).

mies and Seminaries; Academies have become Colleges, and Colleges, Universities. We have 'Athenian warehouses for domestic manufactures'—Lyceums for vending ice-creams; and ere long will probably boast of an Areopagus of Shoeblacks. 'Big men you,' as the Indian said to the white man—and we talk 'big' on occasions that don't require it, giving an air of unnatural consequence to trifles, and very often rendering the most affecting circumstances, as well as the highest achievements, ludicrous, by attempting to bake better bread than can be made of wheat." [6]

Here are two of his literary dicta:

"I believe the perfection of a work of genius to consist in the symmetry and harmony of its parts, the purity of the design, the chastity of its embellishments, and the nice judgment with which the whole is put together." [7]

In February, 1847, he wrote to a friend:

"To be a competent judge of a work, the critic should not only possess the genius of the author, but be his superior in taste and judgment." [8]

In his strictures on romanticism Paulding surpassed Thomas Carlyle, who noted that many of Scott's characters were more showy than real and who advised people to close their Byron and read Goethe. Paulding thought that the chief fault of the romantic poets was their failure to plan and mature their works. Though he liked Scott's charity and geniality, he called him a great second-hand artist, who furbished old material and who owed much of his success to his Tory politics. He praised Miss Edgeworth as a painter of life as it is and Scott as a painter of life as it was. Wordsworth and Coleridge appear to have made little impression upon him. He liked Byron's

[6] *Letters from the South,* Vol. 1, p. 248.

[7] *A Sketch of Old England,* Vol. 1, p. 218.

[8] E. A. Duyckinck Collection, Manuscript Room, New York Public Library.

independence, but he denounced his poems as "harum-scarum fragments," and he declared that Byron had opposed "the cant of religion and philanthropy with that of misanthropy and skepticism." He called Dryden the best critic of modern times. As already noted, for a model novelist he reverted to Fielding; he rated Shakespeare the greatest English author, and Milton the noblest and most inspired of all the English bards. (See *A Sketch of Old England*, Vol. 2, pp. 84–156. Byron is also satirized in "The Poet's Tale," "The Azure Hose," and "The Dunce and the Genius.")

His theory of realism is well illustrated by Cooper's *The Pioneers*, which he admired as a true delineation of characters, manners, and scenery. But one day he heard two smart young fellows pronounce the novel vulgar, the characters low, and the incidents commonplace. After reflection he reached this explanation of their difference in opinion:

"With certain people, perhaps a large portion of those who read novels, every thing which is not fashionable is vulgar. A worthy farmer or mechanic, in a clean white frock, and thick-soled shoes is vulgar, and therefore ought not to be introduced into a novel. In short, with this class of readers and critics, every trait of nature, and every exhibition of manners, or dress, which does not come up to the standard of fashionable elegance, is of necessity low and vulgar.

"If we trace this vulgar error to its source, we shall find it, in general, flowing from a false opinion with regard to what constitutes real refinement. In the general estimation, refinement or gentility, as opposed to vulgarity, consists not in intellectual, or moral superiority, but in outward manners and outward splendors, in station, title, or wealth. This opinion is the offspring of ignorance and vulgarity combined." [9]

Though J. G. Wilson in *Bryant and His Friends* (1886) stated that Paulding was not a poet, Irving was of the

[9] *Koningsmarke*, Vol. 2, pp. 67–71.

opinion that he had poetical thoughts in abundance, but was too impatient of the labor of correction to write long poems. Like Emerson, apparently, he was a poet in the rough, or a poet with an imperfect delivery. Paulding was convinced that poetry should be more than a jingle of words, that it should express ideas.

"One of the best tests of poetry, [he wrote in February, 1847] is to turn it into plain prose, and see how it looks in its nakedness. At present, it is a mere fine lady dressed up in such a profusion of incongruous ornaments, that it is impossible to tell what are her real proportions, or what nature has actually done for her." [10]

Again in the same letter:

"The basis of all good poetry as well as all good writing is common sense."

Accordingly, he was an admirer of Pope's unequalled couplets, which he imitated in *The Backwoodsman*. Yet Paulding was fully aware of Pope's limitations, in that, as the poet of reason, refinement, and philosophy, he made little or no appeal to the feelings and imagination. Pope, Paulding held, was the poet of the understanding without romantic delusions, but Thomson was the poet of youth, nature, and the uncorrupted heart. The truth of Crabbe's realism he doubted; and even were it true, he felt that pictures of vice and depravity were unbecoming the poet's art and tended to inculcate a dislike for the common people. He preferred Thomson, Burns, and Goldsmith, who induce us to love the poor and wish them well.

"We do not read poetry, [he reasoned] to acquire worldly experience, but rather to temper those bitter feelings towards our

[10] E. A. Duyckinck Collection, Manuscript Room, New York Public Library.

fellow creatures, which worldly contests, the collision of interests, and the struggles of ambition, are so apt to inspire." [11]

For the American poets before 1845, Paulding had no high regard. With few exceptions he thought they were weakly imitative, transcendentally obscure, or morbidly affected. As early as 1817 he predicted that American critics would be the last to detect a classical poem when it should appear, and that its fame, as happened with Poe and Whitman, would reverberate to America from the other side of the Atlantic. He consistently bewailed American imitation of foreign costumes, music, and literature; he denounced our want of confidence and self-respect, which, he felt, excited the contempt of foreigners and repressed the genius of our country.

His own poetical efforts were limited to two volumes of verse and to a number of short poems published in the magazines and in his prose works, including the *Literary Life.* His first volume, *The Lay of the Scottish Fiddle,* parodied and imitated Sir Walter Scott's verse stories, advocated the War of 1812, lashed American follies, and presented descriptions of American scenery and manners. The plot is negligible, but the humor has some merit. The poem, which was attributed to Walter Scott, pleased Halleck. A burlesque couplet runs:

> "The fiddle stopped; and sudden rose
> The music of the minstrel's nose."

The Backwoodsman (1818) was Paulding's major poetic experiment, and the first book unluckily that carried the author's name. For five years he pondered over the material, and then he composed it in about 1650 heroic couplets divided into six books. The rambling story tells how

[11] *A Sketch of Old England,* Vol. 2, p. 132.

Basil, the hero, weary of renting, emigrated with his family from New York to the Ohio Valley, where, after overcoming many obstacles and engaging in an Indian war, he attained success and prominence. The poem aims to present a typical pioneer, but is the gloomiest of Paulding's works. Written in a period of ill health, it shows that the author's mind was then occupied with the problem of suffering, evil, and death. One of his most daring conceptions is that of the half-crazed Indian prophet's dying defiance of the Great Spirit, ending,

> "If thou hadst power, why then refuse thine aid?
> If not, then have thy vot'ries idly prayed;
> Thou art a cheat that in the heav'ns dost dwell,
> Take my defiance, and so fare thee well."

Many of the couplets are well turned; for example,

> "And baby sympathy is grown so nice,
> It pampers idleness and pities vice."

> "But where corruption takes a thriving root,
> The plant is soon detected by its fruit."

> "The great peacemaker, Death, makes all men friends,
> The league he signs and sanctions never ends."

But the author was so absorbed in the writing of neat couplets that he almost forgot to tell the story. Besides, though condensed and thoughtful, the verses lack vivacity, and inevitably become monotonous. There is much description of a rather gloomy sort. The *London Monthly Magazine* commended the author's robust energy, but stated that his poetic faculties were not of the highest order. (See also Chap. IV, p. 58.)

Among his lyrics "The Blue Bird" is representative of his defects and merits:

"Whene'er I miss the Blue-bird's chant,
  By yon woodside, his favourite haunt,
  I hie me melancholy home,
  For I know the winter soon will come.

"For he, when all the tuneful race,
  Have sought their wintry hiding place,
  Lingers, and sings his notes awhile,
  Though past is nature's cheering smile,

"And when I hear the Blue-bird sing
  His notes again, I hail the spring;
  For by that harbinger I know,
  The flowers and zephyrs soon will blow.

"Sweet bird! that lovest the haunts of men,
  Right welcome to our woods again,
  For thou dost ever with thee bring
  The first glad news of coming spring." [12]

Paulding's love of and joy in nature were highly poetical. From youth to old age he found delight in observing the wonders of creation. In a sane appreciation of nature he may be compared with Wordsworth himself. In support of this point, let us consider three passages. The first summarizes the benefits conferred by nature; the second records a vivid personal experience, in which he realized the biblical promise made to the pure in heart; the third poetically presents his conception of the Universe.

"The silent solitudes of nature are not the promoters of the guilty passions; it is where the human race herd together in crowds, amid all those luxurious seductions, appealing to the senses and the imagination, through every avenue of the heart, that the passions become epidemical, spreading like contagion from one to another, until the entire mass becomes diseased and corrupted. There is no incitement to sensuality in the charms of nature; no seduction in her music; no mischief in her smiles; no

[12] *Koningsmarke*, Vol. 1, pp. 94–95.

luxurious fascination in the rich bounties she pours out with such a lavish hand; and they who would secure to themselves the cheapest, the purest, and the most enduring source of innocent enjoyment, should cherish in their inmost heart a feeling of admiration for that stupendous and beautiful fabric, which more than any other work of his hand, displays the wisdom, the goodness, and the omnipotence of the great Architect of the universe." [13]

The second passage, coming as it does from a stern realist and a clear thinker, is one of the most remarkable in American literature. In imaginative insight it may be compared with Wordsworth's "Tintern Abbey." The introduction of the mouse, seemingly a blemish, proves that Paulding was in full possession of his faculties.

"The first night I spent in the village [Tarrytown] I could not sleep. Accustomed for years to the fretful racket of a great commercial city, which is never quiet by day or by night, the death-like silence, the dread repose which reigned all around me, conjured up in my mind associations with death and oblivion. It seemed the silence of the grave. I lay and listened for some whisper of life, and the sound of my own breathing startled me. A mouse was rustling about somewhere in the wall, and the awful silence of all the world besides caused the sounds to assume the semblance of some one attempting to open the window. I rose, opened it myself and looked out on a scene so wondrous quiet, yet so lovely, that I forgot the sense of loneliness in communing with the beauties of the earth and the heavens. A delicious, soul-subduing melancholy, associated, yea, mingled with a consciousness that I was standing in the presence of the great Creator of all these wonders, stole over my mind, and that night I received an impression of the divinity, such as all I had ever read or heard had failed to create. The bay lay stretched out before me, as bright and still as the surface of a mirror, insomuch that the very moonbeams slept on it without trembling; a number of vessels with their white sails all standing, lay becalmed on the expanse of the waters; beyond, the opposite shore looked like a shadow of a world; and above, the blue heavens, the

[13] *The Old Continental*, Vol. 1, page 72.

twinkling stars, and the full orbed moon, led irresistibly to the contemplation of a world to come. The rays of a morning sun in the month of June tipt the hills of the western shore with golden luster, before I became conscious that the night was past and the day come." [14]

The third selection is a poem in blank verse, entitled "The Universe God's Temple":

O Nature! thou'rt the Temple of our God!
Thy silence is His voice, thy smile His look,
Thy harmony is His, and all thy excellence
Is but the type of His Omnipotence!

Yon arching sky's the roof of His abode,
Spangled with starry lustres that outshine
All the bright jewels of imperial pride;
The Earth's His footstool, carpeted with flowers,
That throw up incense in their gratitude;

The vast, unwearied, melancholy main,
Boundless and fathomless, that wraps the Earth,
Within its winding sheet of cooling waves,
In its majestic fury speaks His wrath,
And in its calms, His mercy and forgiveness:
The fire that belches from the mountain's womb,
Streaking the angry skies with blood-red hues;
The gale that maddens all the peaceful air,
And sweeps the labor'd works of man away;
The earthquake, and the forked shaft of Heav'n,
Wing'd with a death so swift that none can feel,
All are His slaves that crouch beneath His pow'r,
And do His bidding, without saying nay.
The laws of Nature are the laws of God,
The humble creatures of His sovereign will,
By whose obedient agency He sways
His vast creation of the universe.

[14] From "A Visit to My Native Village after an Absence of Thirty Years," *Southern Literary Messenger*, January, 1837; Vol. 3, pp. 1–5.

> This is His Temple! this the fitting shrine,
> For Man, the great High Priest appointed here,
> The only being who can speak His praise,
> For the dumb beasts, and all inanimate things,
> That have no voice to tell their gratitude,
> To offer up his humble orisons.
> All other Temples are the work of man—
> This—this alone is worthy of his God.[15]

Though neither wholly original nor especially rhythmical, these lines are concrete, picturesque, and sincere. If inferior to the "Nineteenth Psalm" and Bryant's "A Forest Hymn," they are nevertheless poetical and worthy of preservation. They illustrate Paulding's theory that definite thought should be the basis of poetry, and they indicate his kinship as a nature poet to Bryant and Wordsworth. The main idea of the poem is often repeated in his prose descriptions of nature.

But Paulding's poetry and criticism were usually incidental and fragmentary. He did not develop or show his full strength either as poet or as critic. Indeed, he rated creative work so much higher than criticism that he scorned the professional critic. His stricture on the American prose and poetry of a century ago is no less creditable than the commendation that his own prose won from Edgar Allan Poe. His estimate of the great authors is usually sound. That he shared Carlyle's adverse opinion of Byron is noteworthy; that he conceded a pre-eminent position to Shakespeare, Fielding, Milton, and Dryden, and admired Chaucer and Burns will not lower his rating as a critic. As to his theoretical preference of realism to romanticism, Paulding's practice in the composition of his ghost and fairy stories proved that he did not reject the valid claims of romanticism. Perhaps the soundest

---

[15] *The Opal* (annual), 1846, New York, pp. 136–7.

theory is that realism and romanticism are complementary and that the supreme literary achievement is their successful fusion. Is it not true that Homer, Dante, and Shakespeare blend the two? Surely, dreams and vivid imaginings may influence human conduct as powerfully as the facts of history or the conclusions of science.

CHAPTER VIII

SECRETARY OF THE NAVY. RETIREMENT AT HYDE PARK

PAULDING's long connection with the navy culminated in his becoming Secretary of the Navy in President Martin Van Buren's cabinet. He succeeded Mahlon Dickerson, and served from July 1, 1838 to March 4, 1841. To fill the vacancy Van Buren, who was himself an amiable New York Dutchman, sought a New Yorker. He offered the position first to Jacob Sutherland, who declined it chiefly on the ground that the salary of $6000 was inadequate to support his family and to provide for the appropriate social functions. Next, Washington Irving received the offer, and declined it because he felt too sensitive to endure the harsh cares and turmoils of political life in Washington. In May, the President sent an invitation to Paulding, who after some hesitation accepted. In a letter to Andrew Jackson, Van Buren characterized his choice as inflexibly right upon all points, a steadfast friend, and a capable official. Paulding's appointment was acceptable to the South because of his stand on abolition, and after some initial surprise it was generally well received.[1]

His first report to the President indicated the compass of his new duties. His office required a dozen clerks and two messengers. In the American fleet were 47 sailing warships, with 10 under construction, and with a personnel of about 200 officers and 8500 seamen of all classes.

[1] Van Buren Correspondence in Congressional Library.

The total annual outlay was about $5,000,000, of which $100,000 were expended for pensions and $250,000 for new ships. The task of administration was so onerous that Paulding soon ceased to write anything except naval orders. In letters to his friends he graphically described his reactions to the work. He invited them to come and see "a gentleman of leisure metamorphosed into a packhorse"; again he declared himself to be the greatest slave in Washington except the President. After giving a grand dinner that lasted four hours, he observed, "It was voted a great thing, but a few more such victories and Pyrrhus is undone." Accustomed as a novelist to have his characters act according to his will, he expected the same unquestioning obedience from his naval subordinates. So, when Lieut. D. G. Farragut of Civil War fame published a signed article casting doubt and suspicion upon a French officer, he received a sharp reprimand from the Secretary, who elsewhere humorously styled himself "the most absolute of all despots."

Two defects in the navy which Paulding set out to correct were strife and intemperance, which were rendering the service inefficient. Many of the ships he found to be hotbeds of wrangling and bitter animosities among the officers. "Their attention," Paulding wrote, "is so much taken up with the assertion of their rights that they very often forget their duties." He roundly denounced drunkenness as degrading to the men, disgraceful to the service, and dangerous to the country; and he ordered the officers to report every case of intemperance. In harmony with his faith in the virtue of work, he also directed commanders to keep all officers and men employed, to maintain firm discipline, to curtail leave of absence, to encourage thrift and economy, and to refrain from sending communications to the newspapers.

"My young midshipmen and lieutenants too," he wrote in July, 1838, "are extremely bilious at this season of the year, and when I order them in service answer me by a request for permission to accompany mamma to the White Sulphur Springs for their health. I am as you know a pretty obstinate fellow, and have already begun to let them know that these things will no longer be permitted." [2] His chief object, then, was to restore discipline; and in doing so he made many enemies, though the President supported him loyally.

Paulding also proposed several constructive measures. In 1838 he recommended the building of a drydock at New York, because the two at Norfolk and Boston were so inadequate that a dozen ships were lying in the harbors and decaying for want of repairs. He insisted on better training of officers and men. To this end in June, 1839, he approved the placing of a small library on every ship in active service. The list of books he chose is interesting. In addition to technical works and copies of treaties, it included Marshall's *Life of Washington*, Gibbon's *Decline and Fall of the Roman Empire*, *Encyclopaedia Britannica*, Plutarch's *Lives*, Kent's *Commentaries*, the *Bible* and *Prayer Book*, *The Federalist*, Cooper's *The Pilot*, *Red Rover*, *The Water-Witch*, *Homeward Bound*, and *History of the Navy of the United States*, and Irving's *Astoria*.

Since the method of teaching on shipboard and at the navy yards was defective and unsatisfactory, he agreed with his predecessors in earnestly recommending the establishment of a naval academy, which first opened its doors to students at Annapolis, Maryland, in October, 1845, when George Bancroft was Secretary of the Navy. Though Paulding had no taste for the violent and eccentric behavior of steamboilers and all such new-fangled contrivances, he aided the President in choosing a committee, authorized by Congress, to test the usefulness of inventions

2 *Literary Life*, p. 271.

to improve and render safe the boilers of steam engines; and his report for 1839 stated that two steam frigates, also authorized by Congress, had been let to contract. In these cases Congress was leading. It is instructive, also, to note that he sent out two ships to the coast of Africa to suppress an illegitimate slave trade carried on there under the American flag but apparently not by Americans.[3]

The most spectacular undertaking of Paulding's secretaryship was the South Sea Exploring Expedition, which sailed from Norfolk in August, 1838, and returned to New York, in June, 1842. It had been authorized by Congress in May, 1836, but the delays in sailing and the expense were so great that they are said to have caused Paulding's predecessor, Mr. Dickerson, to lose his position. The exploration fleet, under command of Lieut. Charles Wilkes, included six small ships, a dozen scientific experts, and a force of about 650 officers and men. "The expedition," ran Paulding's instructions, "is not for conquest, but discovery. Its objects are all peaceful; they are to extend the empire of commerce and science; to diminish the hazards of the ocean, and point out to future navigators a course by which they may avoid dangers and find safety." The published records of the expedition fill several volumes. The party sailed 85,000 miles, surveyed 280 islands, explored 1500 miles of the Antarctic Continent and 800 miles of the Oregon Coast and rivers, and circumnavigated the globe. With polar icefields and barbarous South Sea natives the crew had many exciting adventures. Lieut. William L. Hudson, in charge of the far-south explorations, penetrated to 70 degrees south latitude off Patagonia and to 65 degrees off New Zealand.[4]

[3] *Officers of Ships of War, No. 28,* Naval Library, Washington, D. C.
[4] Naval Reports of Secretary; *Graham's Magazine,* Vol. 13, p. 164; and *Narrative of U. S. Exploring Expedition.*

In its international aspects Paulding's naval policy was eminently sound.

"The position of the United States, [he reasoned] remote as it is from the scene of European rivalry, affords no immunity from its consequences. Commerce makes neighbors of all nations; and the conflicts of interest or ambition between any two, can scarcely fail of involving many others. Against such imminent contingencies an adequate naval force, keeping pace with the commerce and resources of the country, well manned, and above all, well disciplined, is our most effectual security." [5]

In the presidential election of 1840 the people are reputed to have visited the sins of Jackson upon his political descendant, Martin Van Buren. At all events, after a noisy and picturesque campaign, William H. Harrison and John Tyler were elected. Paulding figured in one of the Tippecanoe song books:

> "And next," says Paulding, "I do wish
>   To novels I had stuck,
> For writing them would ne'er have made
>   Of me so lame a duck.

> "Dea' Matty [Van Buren], we must soon go back
>   To quiet Kinderhook,
> And in your garret I will write
>   Another shilling book." [6]

In spite of political jesters Paulding had been remarkably successful in his political activities. For more than forty years he had served the United States. He had risen from an obscure to a high and responsible station in public life. Though he probably shared Mr. Van Buren's unfulfilled hope of a return to power in 1844, he was willing and prepared to retire. Before returning to New York City,

[5] Paulding's Report, Nov. 30, 1838.

[6] From "The Last Cabinet Council," pp. 45–48 in Tippecanoe Song Book (New York Public Library).

he attended a White House dinner for the incoming and outgoing cabinet officials, who made plenty of noise and feasted on hard cider. To Paulding's satiric eye most of the newcomers resembled arrant rogues!

During the remainder of 1841 he was secluded in New York. For several months Mrs. Paulding had been critically ill, and she died on May 25, 1841. His own health was not good, and altogether the year was depressing. He lived in Hudson Square and wrote occasional editorials for the *New York Evening Post*. The next February, Paulding joined Van Buren in a long tour of 7000 miles through the South and West. From New Orleans to St. Louis they traveled on a steamboat. Paulding enjoyed all of the journey except the interminable parades and receptions. Van Buren made the speeches. On their return they visited both Henry Clay and Andrew Jackson. In *Graham's Magazine*, Paulding later published two sketches suggested by the trip, namely, "The Mississippi" and "The Illinois and the Prairies." He was deeply impressed by the Father of Waters, and delighted with the extent, fertility, and promise of the West.

With health and vivacity restored by the trip, he then enjoyed an Indian Summer of authorship. For a decade he contributed to newspapers and periodicals, publishing stories and essays in *Graham's Magazine, Godey's Magazine* and *The Literary World*. As already shown, he put forth novels in 1846 and 1849. He collaborated with his son William in a volume of undistinguished plays. An incident of this period proves his interest in Chaucer. Having rendered the editor of the *Southern Literary Messenger* some gratifying service, he received a draft for twenty dollars. Afterwards when Paulding was entertaining the editor in his New York home, he took him to his library, showed him a handsome, two-volume, folio edition of Chaucer's works, and graciously stated that the purchase of the books was the most complimentary use he could make of the remittance.[7]

In December, 1844, Paulding wrote Van Buren that he and his sons had decided to remove from the city to a farm, located preferably near the ex-president's estate. Again he confided to him that he hoped to leave his sons ''an income of some thousand dollars.'' But he urged them to be industrious, and advised them to follow their own tastes provided these were innocent and did not interfere with the rights of others. William liked journalism, and two others preferred farming. In April, 1846, their father paid $19,000 in cash for a tract of forty-three acres, with a handsome residence, located seven or eight miles north of Poughkeepsie and one mile north of Hyde Park, between the public road and the Hudson River. The spacious country mansion was on a knoll from which little grassy vales and wooded slopes led gracefully down to the river, and it commanded an enchanting view of the placid Hudson, of the elevated farm lands and wooded hills beyond, and of the Catskill Mountains far off to the north. Irving pronounced it one of the most beautiful prospects along the Hudson. Near-by were fine maples, elms, and locusts, and an occasional hemlock or white pine. Thus surrounded by nature's beauties and the warm hearts of his children, grandchildren, and brother Nathaniel, the aging author settled down to a peaceful and comfortable mode of life. He played at farming, knocked over impudent weeds with his cane, smoked a friendly pipe, wrote a little, amused himself with current follies, fairy tales, and the children, and grew old gracefully.

His last days were also gladdened by interesting visitors

[7] B. B. Minor's *The Southern Literary Messenger* (1905), pp. 117–118.

and pleasant correspondents. Among the callers were Simms, Irving, Van Buren, Tuckerman, Gouverneur Kemble, J. G. Wilson, and E. A. Duyckinck. Paulding seldom traveled farther than Poughkeepsie, but with Van Buren, who lived on a fine estate at Kinderhook, he exchanged witty letters on the delights of farming and the perils of politics. To E. A. Duyckinck, in reply to questions regarding himself and his contemporaries, went autobiographic letters and other data, which are preserved in the New York Public Library. Most pleasant and extended was Paulding's correspondence with Hon. Joseph S. Sims of South Carolina. They never met except through the medium of their letters, some of which are reproduced in the *Literary Life;* but between them sprang up a sincere and beautiful friendship, which lasted to the end of Paulding's life.

In September, 1851, Paulding wrote to a committee of Charleston, South Carolina, in regard to secession, a letter which caused a mild commotion and was widely copied, especially in the South. In it he asserted his belief in the right of states to secede, but withheld his opinion as to its expediency. "South Carolina," he advised, "must act for herself and rely on herself alone." He was strong for voluntary cohesion, but he feared that force could not preserve the Union, since it was voluntarily formed on the basis of perfect equality. In other words, Paulding was a states' rights man. Two years later, he probably composed the inscription for the handsome monument erected in Tarrytown to the memory of André's captors. Certainly, no one then living was better qualified than he to conceive a fitting tribute.

About this time he summed up his happiness in a poem called "The Old Man's Blessings." Among its twenty-two stanzas are the following:

"But trust me, friend, it is not so;
  Age has of joys its hidden store,
As rich as youth can e'er bestow,
  Which memory reckons o'er and o'er.

"Remember that the withered leaf,
  Just ere it falls to rise no more,
Discloses, for a period brief,
  A brighter tint than e'er it wore.

*   *   *   *   *   *   *

"And best of all, a little band
  Of noisy imps climb up my knees,
And ramble with me, hand in hand,
  Along the brook, among the trees.

"Then why should I of age complain?
  If 'tis a punishment to prove,
God would not promise it to man
  As a reward of filial love.

"Content to live, content to die,
  I care not when king death appears;
But, if 'tis God's good pleasure, I
  Don't fear to live an hundred years." [8]

In the last decade of his life, some efforts mere made to republish his works. In 1854, at the request of Charles Scribner, Paulding supplied the Duyckinck brothers with information in regard to his life, books, and miscellaneous writings, and he selected prose specimens, which were published in the Duyckinck *Cyclopaedia of American Literature* (1855). The following letter to Charles Scribner is of considerable interest:

[8] *Literary Life,* pp. 356–358.

"Hyde Park, Duchess County,
"May 15th, 1854.

"Sir,

"I received some days since your printed circular requesting me to furnish you with a sketch of my life; notices of my literary contemporaries; dates of the publication of my writings; articles written for magazines, reviews, etc., etc.

"As to the first, the events of my life have been of the ordinary, commonplace kind and I apprehend would be of little interest to the public. The brief sketch in Putnam's Book is correct and to that I refer you for particulars. With respect to my literary contemporaries, I have had opportunities of forming few intimacies, and am not able to give you any information worth publishing.

"Having no copies of the first editions of my writings, and my memory being not very retentive, I cannot at this distance of time state with any thing like accuracy either their dates or the order of their publication.

"My miscellaneous writings are so numerous and dispersed in so many directions through periodicals and newspapers that it is quite impossible for me to specify one-tenth part of them or direct where they are to be found, as I have procured copies of very few of them. With some I gave my name at the request of the publishers; but by far the greater portion are anonymous, consisting of poems, tales, and political articles, and in fact almost every thing. If collected they would probably form twenty or thirty volumes, a very considerable portion of which I am very willing should be forgotten.

"I am pleased to find you have engaged the Messrs Duyckinck to conduct the work, as I am sure they will do it full justice. If I might be permitted, I would suggest that they give copious extracts from the different authors, which are better than criticisms, and indicate no preference, which always gives more or less offense to some of the *genus irritabile*. I think it would also be well to pay some attention to the writers previous to the Revolution, many of whom, though almost forgotten, are well worth remembering.

"Respectfully
"Your obedt. Servt.,
"J. K. Paulding.

"P. S.—I shall be happy to give the Messrs Duyckinck any information in my power on any subject connected with their work if they will state the particular points."[9]

The next year Paulding sent to his friend, George P. Morris, the following letter, in which he predicted that the basic soundness of his writings would be ultimately recognized:

"Hyde Park Duchess Cty.
"June 4th, 1855.

"My dear General

"I received your letter yesterday and feel much gratified by the friendly interest you take in my behalf.

"From the Harpers I expected nothing; nor do I conceive they have any legal claim over my writings under the old contract. But I don't think it worth my while to enter into a contract with them.

"If you can find any Publisher bold enough to take the risk of buying me out of the hands of the Philistines, I shall be obliged to you, though I don't wish you to urge it on them, as it is very possible it may turn out a bad speculation. I have however not much expectation of your succeeding. I some years ago proposed the thing to Putnam, who declined on the ground that it might give offence to the Harpers.

"As my great object is to rescue my works from that oblivion to which they seem part tending, I am perfectly willing the Publisher—if any can be found—should have the entire proceeds until he is completely remunerated for his expenses in the purchase of the stereotype Plates, which by the way, I cannot help suspecting have been destroyed by fire. I should like very much to ascertain whether it is so or not, and this might be done by some one wishing to see in what condition they are previous to purchasing them.

"In your overtures, or suggestions, to the publishers, you will be pleased to avoid all appearance of anxiety on my part for the publication, and act as only from a friendly solicitude on your part, as is in truth the case. The older I grow, the

[9] Duyckinck Collection, Manuscript Division, New York Public Library.

more indifferent I feel on the subject, being pretty well assured that if my writings have the principle of vitality in them they will revive at some time or other, and if not they cannot be Galvanized into life by any efforts of mine.

"I have been lately much gratified with reading in the last number of the United States Review an article which at length does you justice. It comes somewhat late in the day, but in such cases the later the better. You and I belong to the class of 'Latter day Saints. Though left in the rear in the first heats, we have *good bottom* and I predict, will come in at the last round ahead of some of the 'Eclipses.'

"I hope you will soon find leisure to pay us a visit at Hyde Park, where you will find a hearty welcome. I shall have pleasure in showing you my Place, the situation of which is almost a gnat to yours.

"Very truly your friend,
"J. K. Paulding." [10]

In noting the imperfections of this letter, the reader should remember that it was written by an old man in his seventy-seventh year. Mr. Morris's friendly interest in Paulding, and his overtures to the publishers in his behalf were unavailing.

Few pictures of Paulding have been preserved. He had no vanity, and found sitting for his portrait irksome. His grandson, James K. Paulding, Jr., of New York City, has a portrait painted by Wood, and the descendants of Judge Morris S. Miller of Utica, New York, are said to have a full-sized portrait, representing the author in buff-colored small clothes and white-topped boots.[11] His son William left this pen portrait of him:

"Mr. Paulding, as I recollect him, was a man a little above the medium height, strongly built about the bust and arms,

[10] The original letter, which is reproduced here by permission, is in the Library of Yale University.

[11] Letter to E. A. Duyckinck, Oct. 6, 1854 (New York Public Library).

but not so powerfully in the lower limbs; though, in the early
sports of the Salmagundians, I am told he was noted as a
leaper. In his youth he had soft and fine black hair, but in
his later years was absolutely bald. His complexion was dark,
and his eyes of an unmixed brown. His profile was more
striking than his full face, and might have passed, according
to fancy, for an old Indian chief, or an ancient philosopher.
This was before he allowed his beard to grow, as he did for
some years before his death.'' [12]

The Pauldings had a firm grip on life. Among them
octogenarians were quite the fashion, and some became
nonagenarians. The author was no exception, though
after 1847 his mental powers declined appreciably. With
a composed mind, without fear but not without physical
pain, he slowly yielded to old age. At Hyde Park, New
York, he died on April 6, 1860, in his eighty-second year.
A few days later his body was laid to rest in a still un-
marked grave or vault in Greenwood Cemetery, Brooklyn,
New York.

In his will, drawn in 1852, Paulding disposed of a considerable estate. Indeed, few American authors have
equalled him in business ability. Behind him stretched
sixty years of tireless industry and Dutch economy. His
own savings had been increased by inheritances from his
wife and from his brother Nathaniel. He made safe in-
vestments. Accordingly, the estate that he divided among
his sons, Peter, William, and Gouverneur, was probably
worth fifty to eighty thousand dollars. James N., who
was not mentioned in the will, had been virtually adopted
by a maternal aunt, who was childless. Besides the Hyde
Park property,[13] which Peter sold in 1865 for six thousand

---

[12] *Literary Life,* pp. 380–1.

[13] The Paulding home, called ''Placentia,'' burned down many
years ago, but a picture of it was reproduced in Tuckerman's *Homes
of American Authors* (1853).

dollars more than the cost, the author owned foundry stock and three or four houses in New York. The library he divided among his sons; but his book copyrights and manuscripts he bequeathed to William, who edited a four-volume selection of his father's works in the sixties and compiled the *Literary Life*, which consists principally of letters, poems, and long prose extracts.

When this collection was in preparation, Fitz-Greene Halleck, as we learn from a letter dated March 29, 1867 and preserved in the New York Public Library, recalled his impressions of Paulding in the early days and stated briefly his final estimate of him as a man and a writer. The letter, addressed to Evert A. Duyckinck, who had evidently sent the poet a picture of Paulding, reads in part as follows:

"The likeness of Mr. Paulding does not remind me of him either in his youth or age. I saw him for the first time, I think, in 1813. He was then one of the literary lions of my admiration. In his after life, he honored me with his acquaintance and hospitality.

"I am glad to hear that his collected writings are soon to appear. He had great honor as a writer, and great merit as a man. He thought clearly and bravely, and spoke as he thought. His two lines alluding to our revolutionary soldiers, wherein he says they

'Saved this good land and when the tug was o'er,
Begged their way home at every scoundrel's door,'

are a specimen of his manner of expression when indignantly battling for the right against the wrong." [14]

[14] This extract and another addressed to William I. Paulding were published by Mr. E. A. Duyckinck in an article on Halleck in *Putnam's Magazine* for February, 1868, Vol. 11, p. 238.

CHAPTER IX

SUMMARY AND CONCLUSION

LESS than a century ago James K. Paulding was a prominent figure in American letters. Between 1807 and 1850, he was the friend of political and literary leaders and was himself a versatile author. As collaborator with Irving, defender of the United States, critic, wit, essayist, and author of tales and novels, he became well known and eventually popular. Many of his books were republished in England, and his novels were translated into one or more of the European languages. But on the literary horizon of the twentieth century his figure is only a shadow of its former self. Excepting his part of *Salmagundi*, a condensed edition of *The Dutchman's Fireside*, and a few poems, essays, and tales published in collections of American literature, his writings are now out of print, and he is little read and little known. In competition with later authors and new literary fashions, he has been pushed to the rear. In like manner but to less extent, have Irving, Cooper, and Bryant faded into the past. But fifty years ago there was little prospect that the philosophic realists, Thoreau, Melville, and Whitman, would clamber from the shelf to the center of the literary stage. To what extent Paulding, an older realist, can and should come back is an open question. In the preceding chapters an attempt has been made to show who he was and what he did.

"The world," Paulding remarked to James Grant Wilson in 1858, "has not done me justice. I shall leave my works to posterity and my son William." [1] The statement contains much truth. As an independent critic, he opposed many of the excesses of romanticism, and endeavored to substitute and to popularize the main tenets of a sunny realism. In doing so, he set himself against the current fashion. Though Irving, Poe, Halleck, E. A. Duyckinck, and George P. Morris commended his prose, which the public received favorably, Halleck and Drake criticised his verse, and Willis attacked his prose and called his realism "flat, pointless, and essentially vulgar stuff." A contemporary reply to Willis quoted in the *Southern Literary Messenger* (Vol. 5, p. 417) denounced his criticism as a "malignant attempt to wound the literary reputation of a gifted man." Perhaps Bryant's ill-considered estimate of Paulding's prose in his discourse on Washington Irving was even more damaging. Bryant there asserted that Paulding's later writings were hardly better than his best work in *Salmagundi*. Though the opinion was mistaken and unreasonable, it probably carried great weight in establishing the traditional estimate of Paulding. His son William displayed towards his father's writings a limited knowledge and an unfortunate apologetic attitude, which doubtless encouraged the public neglect. J. G. Wilson's chapter on Paulding, however, in *Bryant and His Friends* (1886) paid tribute to his intellectual robustness, his devoted friendships and hearty hatreds, his joy in sarcasms without malignity, his freedom from illusions of fancy or feeling, his vigorous, ironic language, his love of nature, his patriotism, and characteristic originality. More recently the researches of such scholars as Carl Van Doren and Fred Lewis Pattee have directed attention to Paulding.

[1] *Bryant and His Friends* (1886), p. 152.

Perhaps this study will succeed in removing a few prevalent misconceptions regarding him. The first is that he belongs to the Irving school. It is clear that *Salmagundi* was only a crossroad meeting-place for the two authors. From that point, though they continued to be good friends and sincere admirers of each other's work, they figuratively separated, and each pursued his own way. Irving by inclination and European associations was led to choose the picturesque by-paths of early nineteenth-century romanticism; Paulding, though he was influenced by Scott's charm and power and though he shared the romantic love of nature, preferred in general the firm highway of eighteenth-century realism. In Irving's phrase, they had "distinct and comparative merit." Nor is it true that Paulding's view of life was cynical and splenetic. Though he was critical, realistic, and conservative, he viewed life and portrayed it generously and magnanimously. His good humor was so well founded that it could withstand the floods and storms of reality. Without affectation, his best work is pure, healthful, and wholesome. No one familiar with it will conclude that he wrote nothing worthwhile.

Paulding's sterling character has not been questioned. In his personal life he well-nigh won the blessing promised the pure in heart. Like Wordsworth, he loved and reverenced the whole creation, and he perceived in it the handiwork and presence of God. He was reserved and meditative, and scrupulously just and honest. George Washington was his model of the private and public virtues. His friends, books, and actions testify to his cleanness, sincerity, industry, self-reliance, and discretion. From these traits sprang his fondness for puncturing political, literary, and social shams, and from these traits sprang also his inflexible opposition to the licentious writings of Byron and Moore. He believed that as man thinks, so is he. The integrity of Paulding's character is unquestionable.

Self-reliant, industrious at his writings and in the performance of his official duties, and solitary by inclination and training, Paulding had few close friends. He preferred the objectivity of a spectator. Henry Brevoort wrote Irving of Paulding's secluded habits and the difficulty of getting him into society. His aloofness combined with a satiric tongue and pen would tend to repel strangers. Yet Washington Irving liked him and included him among the lads of Kilkenny, that joyous group of the Salmagundi period; William Irving was close to him and eagerly promoted his interests; George P. Morris was his friend; Edgar A. Poe trusted and praised him; Madison entertained him at his Virginia residence; Van Buren chose him for a companion on his western tour; and, when Paulding retired at Hyde Park, many old friends visited him there and enjoyed his witty comments on past and current events. But with Bryant, Cooper, Halleck, Sands, and Drake, he had only casual associations. He held Bryant to be frigid, Cooper verbose, and Halleck Byronic. Believing that solitude is the nurse of the imagination, Paulding avoided the crowd and kept the noiseless tenor of his way.

His connection with government and literature resembled that of Chaucer, Defoe, and Addison. Out of this association and his patriotism arose his political writings. His heredity and early environment developed an excusable antipathy to the aristocratic rulers of England, though he honored her common people and her great thinkers and writers. In the heyday of Jeffersonian and Jacksonian democracy, he was a democrat, and for a generation he held appointive offices. Of the United States he could truly write:

"I have no other child but thee, my country; and my affections centre in thy bosom. The future is full of anticipations of thy prosperity and happiness. Thy coming greatness dawns upon me in all my moments of thoughtful abstraction; and it is often a subject of serious mortification that I cannot live to see the full fruition of thy glories. I shall be dead and forgotten long before thy progress in arts, science, literature, and all thy peaceful triumphs in the empire of the human mind shall be consummated. But still I look forward with such a strong faith in what shall happen, as sure as the sun shines in the heavens, that the future may almost be said to be present already." [2]

As an author he developed slowly but steadily. He did his best work between the ages of fifty and seventy. He was an independent thinker. He theorized over politics, fiction, prose and poetical style, slavery, states' rights, and other subjects. His active mind and facile pen missed little of contemporary interest, and he was urged on by a strong and persistent impulse to write. The preceding chapters indicate his range and versatility. He was wit and realist, journalist and politician, essayist and poet, philosopher and public official, critic and biographer, and author of tales and novels.

A large portion of his work was journalistic and ephemeral. News, parodies, and satires soon grow old. Except for special students of history and literature, Paulding's political, journalistic, imitative, and satirical writings are dead and forgotten. They served their purpose and passed away. Paulding did not expect them to endure. To a friend he wrote in 1854: "You will infer from this that I have been rather neglectful of my offspring, but the honest truth of the matter is that I considered many of them not worth preserving, and am quite willing they

[2] From "Old Times in New-York," *New York Mirror*, April 30, 1831.

should be forgotten."[3] This process of elimination narrows his output to essays, tales, and novels, many of which may also be discarded. He wrote too much and revised too little; he confused genius and productiveness. In this respect at least he followed the current fashion.

Of more intrinsic worth and enduring interest are some of his essays, a volume of short stories, and two or three novels, especially those of the New York Dutch. Paulding's best work is autobiographic or reminiscent. In the tales and novels of the Dutch he is more trustworthy, though less enchanting, than either Cooper or Irving, because he had more accurate knowledge of Dutch characters and their native eccentricities. His contribution to the short story is perhaps the most significant part of his work. The essays on "National Literature" and "Washington and Napoleon," the tales of "Cobus Yerks," "The Ghost," and "The Magic Spinning Wheel," and the novel, *The Dutchman's Fireside,* are fairly representative of his better writings. To these and similar work, one may safely apply E. A. Duyckinck's opinion written sixty-five years ago:

"When the productions of Paulding, now for some time hidden from the world, shall be revived, the public will find in them, a freshness and interest, a spirit and humor, unabated since their first appearance. To the inhabitants of New York in particular, they will present strong claims to attention, for the author, though he turned his back upon the city, was a genuine son of Manhattan."[4]

[3] J. K. Paulding to E. A. Duyckinck, Oct. 15, 1854, Duyckinck Collection, MS Room, New York Public Library.

[4] Preface to 1860 Edition of *Salmagundi.*

BIBLIOGRAPHY OF JAMES K. PAULDING

I. SEPARATE WORKS

1807–8. Salmagundi; or, the Whim-Whams and Opinions of
Launcelot Langstaff, Esq. and Others. [First series. With
Washington and William Irving. 20 numbers, Jan. 24,
1807–Jan. 25, 1808.] 2 vols. New York, 1807–1808, D.
Longworth. 2 vols. in one with an Introductory Essay
and Explanatory Notes by John Lambert, London, 1811.
A New and Improved Edition in 2 vols. New York, 1814,
David Longworth. Third Edition, New York, 1820, Thomas
Longworth and Co. London, 1823, Tegg. London, 1824,
J. Limbird, with a portrait of Washington Irving. 2
vols. Paris, 1824, A. and W. Galignani. New Edition,
corrected and revised by the author, London, 1824, T.
Davidson; handsomely bound; Paulding's part acknowl-
edged. London, MDCCCXXX, John Murray. A New
Edition, corrected by the authors, New York, 1835, Harper
& Brothers as vols. 1 and 2 of Paulding's Works. Glas-
gow, 1838. New Edition, London, 1839, T. Tegg; 1841,
Charles Daly; 1847, Tegg. Three British editions in 1850:
Tegg; Routledge; and H. Bohn. New York, 1857, Putnam
& Co.; also, 1857, as vol. X of Irving's Works; same, 1859.
Printed from the original edition, with a preface and notes
by Evert A. Duyckinck, New York, 1860, 1867, 1869, and
1861–1864 as vol. XXII of the Works of Washington Irving. Philadelphia, 1870, 1871, and 1872, J. B. Lippin-
cott & Co. from the original edition, with a preface and
notes by E. A. Duyckinck. Philadelphia, 1873. London,
1883, Bell & Son in Bohn's Series. New York, 188?,
Belford Company. New York and London, 1897, in Knickerbocker ed. of Irving's Works. New York, 190?, Thomas
Y. Crowell & Co. New York, 1902, in Hudson ed. of
Irving's Works, with preface and notes by E. A. Duyckinck. Note: Salmagundi was not included in the Works
of Washington Irving pub. by Putnam & Co. in 1848–1851.
TRANSLATIONS: According to Quérard's La France
Littéraire, Vol. 6, p. 637, Paris, 1834, parts of Salmagundi
were translated into French. Swedish, second edition,
Stockholm, 1872.

1812. The Diverting History of John Bull and Brother Jonathan, by Hector Bull-Us, New York, and Philadelphia, 1812, Inskeep & Bradford; and Bradford & Inskeep. Second Edition, New York, 1813, Inskeep and Bradford. London, 1813, Sherwood, Neely, and Jones. Third Edition, Philadelphia, 1819, M. Carey and Son. Third Edition, Improved, Philadelphia, 1827, Robert Desilver. New Edition, New York, 1835, Harper & Brothers as Vol. IX of Paulding's Works. London, 1851. New York, 1867, edited by W. I. Paulding in a volume entitled The Bulls and the Jonathans.

1813. The Lay of the Scottish Fiddle; A Tale of Havre de Grace, supposed to be written by Walter Scott, Esq., New York and Philadelphia, 1813, Inskeep & Bradford, and Bradford & Inskeep. London, A Poem in Five Cantos, Supposed to be written by W—— S——, Esq., First American, from the Fourth Edinburgh Edition, 1814, printed for James Cawthorn.

1815. The United States and England: Being a Reply to the Criticism on Inchiquin's Letters, Contained in the Quarterly Review for January, 1814. Philadelphia, 1815, Bradford and Inskeep, and A. H. Inskeep, New York.

1817. Letters from the South, Written during an Excursion in the Summer of 1816, by the author of John Bull and Brother Jonathan, etc., 2 vols., New York, 1817, James Eastburn & Company. New Edition, by A Northern Man, New York, 1835, Harper and Brothers as Vols. V and VI of Paulding's Works.

1818. The Backwoodsman: A Poem, by J. K. Paulding, Philadelphia, 1818, M. Thomas. [The *New York Mirror* of August 20, 1831, stated editorially that *The Backwoodsman* had been translated into French and German, but no copies have been found.]

1819–20. Salmagundi, Second Series, by Launcelot Langstaff, Esq., Philadelphia, 1819–1820, M. Thomas, and New York, J. Haly and C. Thomas, in fortnightly numbers from June, 1819 to September, 1820. London, 1824. New York, 1835,

2 vols., Harper & Brothers as Vol. III and IV in Paulding's Works.

1822. A Sketch of Old England by A New-England Man, 2
vols., New York, 1822, Charles Wiley. London, 1822, republished in Vol. VIII of Sir R. Phillips' New Voyages
and Travels.

1823. Koningsmarke, The Long Finne, A Story of the New
World, 2 vols., New York, 1823, pub. anonymously by
Charles Wiley. London, 3 vols., 1823. New edition, re-
vised and corrected, 2 vols., New York, 1836, Harper &
Brothers as Vol. VII and VIII of Paulding's Works. Lon-
don, 1839, J. Cunningham, bound in Vol. V of a collection
entitled The Novel Newspaper; authorship attributed to
"Dr. Paulding." London, 1843, 3 vols., Whittaker.
TRANSLATION: German, 2 vols., Frankfurt, 1840.

1825. John Bull in America; or, The New Munchausen, New
York, 1825, Charles Wiley. Second Edition, New York,
1825, Charles Wiley. London, 1825, John Miller. These
editions were anonymous. Edited by William I. Paulding
in a volume entitled The Bulls and the Jonathans and published by Charles Scribner and Company, New York, 1867.

1826. The Merry Tales of the Three Wise Men of Gotham,
edited by the author of John Bull in America, New York,
1826, G. and C. Carvill. New York, Harper and Brothers,
1839.

1828. The New Mirror for Travellers, and Guide to the Springs,
by an Amateur, New York, 1828, G. and C. Carvill. [Since
the title was misunderstood, it was altered to read] The
New Pilgrim's Progress. Edited by W. I. Paulding, with
the original title and eight other tales, and pub. by Charles
Scribner and Co., New York, 1868, in a vol. entitled The
Book of Vagaries.

1829. Tales of the Good Woman, by A Doubtful Gentleman,
New York, 1829, G. and C. and H. Carvill; contained The
Yankee Roué, The Drunkard, Dyspepsy, and Old Times in
the New World. New Edition, in 2 vols., New York, 1836,
Harper & Brothers as Vols. X and XI of Paulding's

Works; Vol. X included Memoir of the Unknown Author, The Yankee Roué, The Drunkard, and Dyspepsy; Vol. XI, The Cradle of the New World, The Politician, and The Dumb Girl. Edited by W. I. Paulding in 1 vol., containing An Introduction by the Editor, Memoir of the Unknown Author, The Azure Hose, The Dumb Girl, Dyspepsy, The Progress of the Age, The Revenge of St. Nicholas, Cobus Yerks, The Ride of St. Nicholas, and The Politician; New York, 1867, Charles Scribner and Co.

1830. Chronicles of the City of Gotham from the papers of A Retired Common Councilman, containing The Azure Hose, The Politician, and the Dumb Girl; edited by the author of The Backwoodsman, Koningsmarke, John Bull in America, etc., New York, 1830, G. and C. and H. Carvill.

1830. The Lion of the West, 1830, a prize-winning comedy never published but often produced successfully in the United States by Mr. James H. Hackett between 1831 and 1850; and in 1833 produced by Mr. Hackett at the Covent Garden theatre in London under the title A Kentuckian's Trip to New York in 1815.

1831. The Dutchman's Fireside, A Tale, by the author of Letters from the South, etc., 2 vols., New York, 1831, J. and J. Harper. London, 1831, 2 vols., Henry Colburn and Richard Bentley. Fifth Edition, same as Vols. XII and XIII of Paulding's Works, New York, 1837, J. and J. Harper. New York, 1838, 2 vols., J. and J. Harper. London, 1839. New York, 1845, 2 vols. in one, Harper and Brothers. New Edition, London, 1849, Routledge. London, 1852. Edited in 1 vol. by William I. Paulding, New York, 1868, Charles Scribner and Company. School Edition, condensed, in the Standard Literature Series, New York, Boston, and New Orleans, 1900, University Publishing Company.

TRANSLATIONS: Translated into French by Mme. A. Sobry, Paris, 1832. Trans. into Swedish, 1833. Trans. into German by Karl Andree, Leipzig, 1837; another German translation, Frankfurt, 1838. Trans. into Dutch, Amsterdam, 1838, pub. by R. L. Klinkert. Trans. into Danish by O. F. Braemer, Copenhaven, 1838.

1832. Westward Ho! A Tale by the author of The Dutch-
man's Fireside, etc., 2 vols., New York, 1832, J. and J.
Harper as Nos. XXV and XXVI in Harper's Library of
Select Novels. London, 1833, 3 vols., entitled The Banks
of the Ohio, or Westward Ho! A Tale by Mr. Paulding,
pub. for A. K. Newman and Company. Another English
Edition in 2 vols., 1833. New York, 1845, 2 vols. in one,
Harper and Brothers.
TRANSLATIONS: Trans. into French by Mme. A. Sobry,
2 vols., Paris, 1833. Trans. into German by Karl Andree,
Leipzig, 1836. Another German translation, 2 vols. in
one, Frankfurt, 1837.

1832. Tales of Glauber-Spa: By Several American Authors,
2 vols., New York, J. and J. Harper, 1832. Of the eight
stories two were by Paulding, namely, Childe Roeliffe's
Pilgrimage in Vol. I and Selim in Vol. II. Childe Roeliffe's
Pilgrimage was separately published in England, 1833.
In the Harper edition of 1844 (New York) the tales were
assigned to Miss C. M. Sedgwick, J. K. Paulding, W. C.
Bryant, R. C. Sands, and William Leggett. Same, two
vols. in one, New York, Harper and Brothers, 1856.

1835. A life of Washington, 2 vols., Harper & Brother, New
York, 1835. Published as Nos. 75 and 76 in Harper's
Family Library, New York, 1836. Harper & Brothers,
New York, 1840, 1841, 1842, and 1845. Pub. by George
Clark and Son, Aberdeen, 1848. New York editions in
1852, 1854, 1858, and 1871.

1836. Slavery in the United States, New York, 1836, Harper
and Brothers.

1836 The Book of Saint Nicholas, New York, Harper and
or   Brothers, 1836 [or 1837; on doubt as to year of publica-
1837. tion see Literary Life, p. 263]. This book was a collection
of ten stories all of which except one had been previously
published in periodical literature. The stories were: The
Legend of St. Nicholas, The Little Dutch Sentinel of the
Manhadoes, Cobus Yerks, A Strange Bird in Nieuw Amsterdam, Claas Schlaschensclinger, The Revenge of St.
Nicholas, The Origin of Baker's Dozen, The Ghost, The

Nymph of the Mountain, and The Ride of St. Nicholas on New Year's Eve.

1838. A Gift from Fairy Land, New York, 1838, D. Appleton and Co. Also pub. under the title A Christmas Gift from Fairyland. Pub. in London, 1840, with one hundred fanciful embellishments.

1846. The Old Continental: or, The Price of Liberty, 2 vols., Paine and Burgess, New York, 1846. Second New York edition by Cady and Burgess, New York, 1851. Also, New York, 1855–1858.
TRANSLATION: Into German, 3 vols., Leipzig, c. 1852–1857.

1847. American Comedies. By J. K. Paulding and William Irving Paulding, Philadelphia, 1847, Carey and Hart.

1849. The Puritan and His Daughter, 2 vols., Baker and Scribner, New York, 1849. Same, New York, 1849. Same, New York, 1850. Two London editions in 1849.
TRANSLATION: Into German, 2 vols., 1850.

II. CONTRIBUTIONS TO PERIODICALS

(Note. For a complete list of Paulding's tales from both book and periodical literature, arranged in chronological order, with date and place of publication and with brief explanatory notes, see Chapter 5, pp. 88–92.)

THE ANALECTIC MAGAZINE (Monthly, Philadelphia)

1813: January–June, "Biographical Notice of Captain Isaac Hull," "Biography of Commodore Decatur"; July–December, Review of Charles Phillips' "The Emerald Isle," "Biography Captain Jacob James," "Cupid and Hymen—An Allegory," Selections from "The Lay of the Scottish Fiddle" with an Introduction by Washington Irving.

1814: January, "Biographical Sketch of the Late Lieutenant Aylwin," "Walbridge" (A Story), "The Battle of Erie" (Verse); February, "The Idea of a True Patriot"; May, "Americanisms"; July, Review of "A General History of

Connecticut''; August, "The Lost Traveler" (A Story);
"May-Day."

1815: September, "The American Naval Chronicle"; Oc-
tober, "The Adventures of Henry Bird," "The Navy";
November, "Biographical Notice of Captain James Biddle";
December, "The Naval Chronicle."

1816: January, "Naval Chronicle" Captain Lewis War-
rington, and Official Documents, "A Sailor's Elegy on the Fate
of the Wasp" (Verse); February, "Naval Chronicle—Sketch
of the Barbary States"; March, "Captain Thomas Mac-
Donough"; April and May, "Synopsis of Naval Actions";
June, "British Record Reviewed"; July, "Naval Chronicle—
Life of John Paul Jones"; August and September, "Synopsis
of Naval Action"; October, "Naval Chronicle."

1817: March and April, "Letters from Virginia."

1819: May, "Biographical Notice of the Late Captain
Thomas Gamble."

THE NORTH AMERICAN REVIEW (Boston)

1815: May, Review and Copious Extracts of "The United
States and England, being a reply to the criticism on Inchiquin's Letters" (From Paulding's book of the same name).

NEW YORK MIRROR (Weekly)

1824: December 18, "An Essay on Love" (Probably Paulding's).

1825: September 10, "Brother Jonathan."

1828: November 29, "Un Fainéant," reprinted from *The
Atlantic Souvenir.*

1829: October 17, "The Ghost," reprinted from *The Atlantic Souvenir.*

1830: August 21, "The Angel of Time"; October 23, "The
Eve of St. Andrew," reprinted from *The Atlantic Souvenir*;
November 20, "Legend of the Ancient Tile-roofed Cottage."

1831: January 1, "Knickerbocker's Hall, or the Origin of Baker's Dozen," "Killing No Murder"; January 15, "American Scenery—New York," "A Trip to Paris," "Want of Excitement or a Trip to London"; January 15 to May 28 "Scraps from My Commonplace Book"; January 22, "The Malaprops"; February 19, "The History of Uncle Sam and His Boys"; February 26, "Simplicity" and "Societies"; March 12, "The Victim of Trifles"; March 19, "Old 76"; April 9, "The Circle of Human Wishes"; April 16, "The Nymph of the Mountain"; April 30, "Old Times in New York," "Time and Truth—An Apologue"; May 14, "A Legend of St. Nicholas"; June 18, "Jonathan's Visit to the Celestial Empire"; August 6, "The Great Medicine or the Magic Whiskers"; September 17, "Manners and Morals—A True Story"; September 25, "The Mother's Choice" (Story); October 1, "Haschbasch the Pearl Diver"; November 19, "Forty Years Ago"; December 31, "The Revenge of St. Nicholas."

1832: March 10, "Too Fast and Too Slow"; July 7, "The History of Uncle Sam and his Womankind"; December 29, "Day and Night or the Water-carrier of Damascus."

1833: February 2, "Claas Schlaschenschlinger"; July 6, "Musa or the Reformation"; December 28, "Adam and Eve."

1834: February 1, "Fables and Allegories"; April 12, "Fables, Allegories and Quaint Remarks"; May 3, "Yankee Pedagogues and Dutch Damsels"; June 7, "Journal of a Late Traveler to the Moon"; July 5, "Shooting Stars"; July 5, "Journal of a Traveler to the Moon"; December 27, "A Story for the Holidays," or "A Strange Bird in Nieuw Amsterdam."

1841: January 2 and 9, "The Nameless Old Woman."

THE ATLANTIC SOUVENIR (Annual, Philadelphia)

1826: "The Eve of St. John"; "A Tale of Mystery"; "The Spanish Girl of the Cordilleras."

1827: "The White Indian"; "The Little Dutch Sentinel of the Manhadoes."

1828: "The Poet's Tale"; "Cobus Yerks."

1829: "Un Fainéant"; "Benhadar."

1830: "The Ghost."

1831: "The Eve of St. Andrew."

1832: "The Dunce and the Genius."

1836: "The Magic Spinning Wheel."

THE KNICKERBOCKER MAGAZINE (Monthly, New York)

1833: January, "A Ramble in the Woods on Sunday"; March, "Running Against Time—A Tale."

SOUTHERN LITERARY MESSENGER (Monthly, Richmond)

1834: August, "Memory and Hope" (Copied from *New York Mirror*).

1836: July, "Example and Precept"; August, "Judgment of a Rhadamanthus," "The Old Man's Carousal" (Verse).

1837: January, "A Visit to My Native Village after an Absence of Thirty Years" (Autobiographical).

1843: January, "The White and the Red Man" (Verse).

THE UNITED STATES MAGAZINE AND DEMOCRATIC REVIEW (Washington)

1838: March, "The School of Reform—A Domestic Tale."

GRAHAM'S MAGAZINE (Monthly, Philadelphia)

1843: March, "The End of the World—A Vision"; April, "The Mississippi"; June, "Too Late and Too Early—Written in 1813"; July, "Lament of the Faithless Shepherdess" (Verse); September, "The Millionaire—A Tale of the Times."

1844: January, "The History of a Lion" (Story); February, "The Old Skinflint Fairy and Her Goddaughter"; June, "The Two Clocks" (Story); July, "Poor Genevieve"; August, "Washington and Napoleon"; September, "Murad the Wise."

1845: January, "The Blind Fiddler of New Amsterdam"; February, "Recollections of the Country."

1846: February and March, "The Mother's Tragedy"; May, "The New Science or the Village Bewitched"; June, "The Vroucolacas—A Tale."

1847: January, "Musa or the Pilgrim of Truth."

1848: January, "The Little Gold Fish—A Fairy Tale"; June, "The Double Transformation."

1849: January, "The Illinois and the Prairies."

GODEY'S MAGAZINE AND LADY'S BOOK (Monthly, Philadelphia)

1846: September, "Jane M'Crea—A Ballad"; October, "Retiring from the Cares of Life"; December (Same, continued).

1847: February (Same, concluded); January, "The Man Whom Everybody Pitied"; June, "Fairy Land and Fairy Lore."

THE LITERARY WORLD (Weekly, New York)

1851: July 19, "Happiness," "Rencontre Island" (Verse).

1852: December 18, "The Old Man's Blessing," "Body and Soul—A Tale."

1853: January 15, "Truth and Falsehood"; February 12, "The Snow Storm" (Verse).
(The preceding published under title: "Odds and Ends.")

HARPER'S MAGAZINE (Monthly, New York)

1915: November, "An Interview with Napoleon's Brother from an Unpublished MS. by James K. Paulding. Edited by James Kirke Paulding" (Grandson).

III. COLLECTED WORKS

New York, Harper and Brothers, 1835–1837, fourteen volumes, containing Salmagundi (First and Second Series), Letters from the South, Koningsmarke, The Diverting History of John Bull and Brother Jonathan, Tales of the Good Woman (six short stories), The Dutchman's Fireside, and The Book of St. Nicholas (ten tales). [Scarce. Set in the library of the New York Historical Society.]

New York, Charles Scribner and Company, 1867–1868, four volumes, containing The Bulls and the Jonathans, Tales of the Good Woman (eight short stories), A Book of Vagaries (The New Mirror for Travellers, and eight tales and sketches), and The Dutchman's Fireside. Selected and edited by the author's son, William Irving Paulding, and accompanied by the Literary Life of James K. Paulding (1867).

IV. BIOGRAPHY, SPECIMENS, AND CRITICISM

Appleton's Cyclopaedia of American Biography, edited by J. G. Wilson and John Fiske.

The Atlantic Club-Book: Being Sketches in Prose and Verse by Various Authors, New York, 1834, 1847; London (no date). Dedicated to James K. Paulding and included his "Jonathan's Visit to the Celestial Empire" and "Knickerbocker-Hall, or The Origin of Baker's Dozen."

BARR, JAMES. *The Humour of America,* with an introduction, London and New York, 1894. Contains Paulding's "The Revenge of St. Nicholas."

The Beauties of Brother Bull-Us by his loving Sister Bull-A, New York, 1812.

BREVOORT, HENRY. *Letters to Washington Irving,* 1916.

The Cambridge History of American Literature, New York, 1917, 1918. See indices of volumes 1 and 2.

DUYCKINCK, E. A. and G. L. *Cyclopaedia of American Literature,* Philadelphia, 1855. Contains a valuable sketch of Paulding's life.

Fraser's Magazine (English), December, 1832 (Vol. 5, pp. 336–350).

GRISWOLD, R. W. *The Prose Writers of America,* Philadelphia, 1847.

Homes of American Authors, 1852.

IRVING, WASHINGTON. *Life and Letters by P. M. Irving,* 1862–64, and *Letters to Henry Brevoort,* 1915.

Knickerbocker Magazine on Paulding's death, July, 1860, and on his writings, January, 1863.

LAMBERT, JOHN. Introduction to London edition of *Salmagundi,* 1811.

Love Tales, American, London and Philadelphia, 1891. Contains "The Little Dutch Sentinel of the Manhadoes."

The Monthly Review (London), August, 1811.

National Intelligencer (Washington), January 17, 1815.

New York Mirror: November 1, 1823; March 19, 1825; May 16, 1829; June 4, 1831; August 20, 1831; May 5, 1832; October 20, 1832.

The North American Review: May, 1815; September, 1819.

PATTEE, FRED LEWIS. *The Development of the American Short Story,* New York, 1923.

PAULDING, WILLIAM I. *Literary Life of James K. Paulding,* New York, 1867.

POE, EDGAR ALLAN. Review of Paulding's A Life of Washington in *Southern Literary Messenger* (1835).

The Quarterly Review (London): January, 1814; January, 1824.

The Scotsman, or Edinburgh Political and Literary Journal, January 22, 1823.

Specimens of the American Poets; with critical notices and a preface, London, 1822.

VAN DOREN, CARL. *The American Novel,* New York, 1921.

WEGELIN, OSCAR. *A Bibliography of the Separate Publications of James Kirke Paulding, Poet, Novelist, Humorist, Statesman, 1779–1860.* Printed in the Papers of the Bibliographical Society of America, vol. 12, Nos. 1–2, January, April, 1918. Contains several inaccuracies.

Western Monthly Magazine, September, 1835. Review of Paulding's collected works reprinted in *New York Mirror* for October 3, 1835.

The Westminster Review (London), October, 1831.

WILLIS, N. P. Criticism of Paulding reprinted from *The Corsair* in *Southern Literary Messenger* for June, 1839. Followed by Mr. Webb's reply in *New York Courier and Enquirer.*

WILSON, JAMES GRANT. *Bryant and his Friends: Some Reminiscences of the Knickerbocker Writers.* New York, 1886.

V. PAULDING APOCRYPHA

Among the books mistakenly attributed to James K. Paulding by some bibliographers are the following:

Jokeby, a Burlesque on Rokeby, Boston, 1813. In a letter dated October 6, 1854, addressed to E. A. Duyckinck, and preserved in the Duyckinck Collection in the New York Public Library, Paulding wrote: "I am not the author of Jokeby and cannot say who is."

Crystalina, A Fairy Tale, New York, 1816. No evidence of Paulding's authorship.

Letters from Virginia Translated from the French, Baltimore, 1816. The Boston Public Library in making this assignment probably confused this book with Paulding's Letters from the South (New York, 1817).

Letter on the Use and Abuse of Incorporations, New York, 1827 (a pamphlet of 59 pages). No evidence of Paulding's authorship.

Affairs and Men of New Amsterdam in the time of Governor Peter Stuyvesant, by J. Paulding, New York, 1843. This book was not claimed by James K. Paulding, and its style clearly indicates that he was not the author.

The First of the Knickerbockers, A Tale of 1673, New York, 1848. No evidence of Paulding's authorship.

The King of the Hurons, New York, 1850. Rejected for the same reason.

So far as known, neither James K. Paulding nor his son William ever claimed these books. The internal evidence of style and matter also tends to confirm their silent rejection.

INDEX